DICKIE HENDERSON
on RADIO and TELEVISION

Compiled and Edited by
Aaron Brown, Simon Coward,
Richard Down and Chris Perry

With career essay by
Graham McCann

ISBN 978-1-900203-86-9

Dickie Henderson on Television and Radio

Kaleidoscope Publishing
42 Victoriana Way
Handsworth Wood
B20 2SZ
United Kingdom

www.tvbrain.info
info@tvbrain.info

DICKIE HENDERSON

by Graham McCann

Dickie Henderson was not merely a star but rather a whole constellation of talents. A show business polymath, a microcosm of multiple media, he could baffle those prone to pigeonholing (and if you don't fit neatly within one or other category, you are in danger of being overlooked or undervalued by all), while delighting those content to appreciate creativity without any classificatory constraints.

To a few impetuously dismissive people, there were two things about Dickie Henderson with which they could never quite come to terms. One was that, thanks both to the nature of his background and the nuances of his sound and style, he seemed neither entirely British nor American but rather blandly mid-Atlantic, and the other was that he was not his more innovative father, Dick Henderson. He struck them, in short, as too elusive a personality, and too derivative a performer, for them to love rather than merely like.

To many others, however, these were two of the several things that helped make him such a memorably versatile and engagingly effective entertainer. Mixing English grit with American glamour, he could be earthy and ironic and mockingly self-aware, but could also be polished and elegant and effortlessly slick, and, thanks to the historic arts and insights handed down from his distinguished father, he had a greater depth of heritage to dip into than any of his contemporaries possessed.

There was, indubitably, something very worldly, and very wise, about Dickie Henderson. It was not just that he always had an air of someone who had already been there and done it. It was also the fact that he had grown up around so many people who had already been there and done it.

He always seemed older than his years, and more experienced than his peers. He did so because of the rich and varied forces that had formed him.

The most central, and strongest, of these forces was his father. Dick Henderson was, in his own right, one of the most intelligent and influential comic performers of his generation. One cannot appreciate the achievements and appeal of Henderson Jnr without first doing so for those of Henderson Snr.

Born on 20th March 1891 in a cramped little house on Strawberry Street at Drypool, Sculcoates, in Kingston-upon-Hull, in the East Riding of Yorkshire, Dick Henderson entered into a working-class world of hard graft and dogged dreams. The son of a planing machinist and a dressmaker, he was only afforded the most basic of education before being sent out to work as an apprentice fitter at the local Earles Shipyard, but, gifted with a powerful voice and a natural wit, he felt far more inclined to entertain.

Starting in the clubs and pubs scattered along the docklands, he was torn between telling funny stories and singing emotive songs, and so ended up doing a bit of both. He once rode on his bicycle the sixty-odd miles from Hull to Leeds for an audition, joined a pierrot troupe at Withernsea, was then recruited to be one of the resident comics in a touring revue, and by the summer of 1914 he was in London, making his debut there at the Canning Town Imperial Theatre (and was judged an instant 'hit' by one local reporter).

War intervened before he could progress any further, and he served for the duration in the Navy, but once discharged in 1918 he returned to the music halls and wasted no time at all in restoring his momentum. Image-conscious right from the start, and driven to develop his own distinctive material, he knew exactly how to make his mark in a crowded market.

Billed for most of his career as 'The Yorkshire Comedian,' he was short (about five feet six) and stout (about sixteen stone), wore a black bowler hat several sizes too small for his head, and a natty blue suit that hung back as if in thrall to the size of his paunch, smoked a stocky sausage of a cigar and affected a chubby, cheery, cherry-cheeked pose that prompted some observers to liken him to John Bull or Mr Punch. Recognition humour was his style, and domestic scenes were his themes, ranging from the difficulties of filling his fountain pen in public to his wife's struggles with the false teeth that were actually made for the mouth of her sister.

The Manchester Guardian called him 'a master of his line': 'He can serve you up the joke that goes straight to anybody's sense of humour, or slip in one that reaches you indirectly and passes you by if you are not alert.'

Unusually self-aware, he was not afraid to acknowledge, and mock, the mechanics of his medium. Originating the phrase 'joke over,' he would tick-off the more laboured of his laughs as if they were commercial breaks interrupting his natural patter. Whereas many comics of the time could seem like machines clicking and clanking out the gags, there was always evidence that Henderson had a brain that was buzzing away throughout the performance.

One of the most novel and influential aspects of his act – Frankie Howerd would be one of those comedians indebted to him in this respect – was his readiness to defy the convention that the performer should strain to entertain. Henderson, in contrast to most of his contemporaries, used to delight in pretending that he was merely going through the motions. 'No, no, please,' he would protest, 'I don't want any applause. I'm strictly doing this for the money. And I've just been paid in advance, so I'm really flogging a dead horse. Don't expect too much.'

He was also unusual, for that era, in being a comedian who sang 'straight' songs – and sang them extremely well. Dickie Henderson (speaking to the author Roger Wilmut for his book *Kindly Leave the Stage!*) would later reflect on this part of his father's performance: 'A lot of people have said that he was responsible some dreadful acts, because he finished with a [straight] song...and then [other comedians] came along afterwards and finished with a song, and *they* really couldn't sing, and so you had these awful comedian-singers; but there's no doubt that Dad was the first'.

Often accompanied by an orchestra, he sometimes surprised the audience by singing from the wings, sounding like a sober-suited serenader, and then would stroll on looking disarmingly droll. Always ready to adapt to match a mood, he drew from a repertoire that ranged from cheerful crowd pleasers such as 'She Can Make A Nice Cup Of Tea' and 'I Want A Pie With A Plum In It,' on to more romantic ballads as 'All My Dreams Are Of You' and 'Since I Found You,' and through to such darker emotional epics (he called them 'sob extractors') as 'I Wish I Had Died In My Cradle (Before I Grew Up To Love You)' and 'Will the Angels Play Their Harps For Me?'.

The song with which he would come to be most closely associated was Al Dubin and Joe Burke's infectious warble of whimsy 'Tip-Toe Thru The Tulips With Me'. Published in 1929, Henderson was one of the first to sing it, and the number proved so popular with audiences that he took to opening and closing many of his performances with it, accompanying himself on a ukulele in a style that would later be emulated by the American singer Tiny Tim.

Some contemporaries would say that, backstage, he could, like many other comedians, appear 'preoccupied and unsmiling' as he safeguarded his energies and sorted through his thoughts, but, as one fellow performer would recall, 'in a bar or otherwise off-duty he could be a vivacious, stimulating companion'. He was a kind and generous man, always supportive of other talents, but there was no doubting, in those early days, the arc of his ambition. Never one to settle for the safety of satisfying a niche, he was set on amusing a mass audience.

1926 would be particularly significant year in the burgeoning career of Henderson Snr. He achieved national fame when he not only made his debut on radio (with his own half-hour special on the BBC) but also appeared in his first Royal Variety Performance, held on 27th May at the London Alhambra and broadcast live (for the first time), in the presence of King George V and Queen Mary. According to one report of the reception of his own routine, the King smiled at and applauded many of his comic lines (including one comparing a flapper to a bungalow: 'They are both painted in front, shingled at the back, and have nothing in the attic') while 'the Queen burst into unrestrained laughter and rocked to and fro in merriment'.

Buoyed by all the critical acclaim (and the commercial consequences – his rate of pay shot up so high that he was now able to travel in Daimlers driven by chauffeurs with peaked caps and gaiters), he then resolved to test his talents beyond the boundaries of Britain. Declaring at the start of the following year that the domestic music hall circuit was now 'on the wane,' he announced that he was setting off in the summer to try his luck in the two other 'competitive markets' still available to an entertainer: Australia and the United States of America.

Accompanied by his wife, Winifred (a stylish Liverpool-born soubrette of Irish descent), and their seven-year-old twin daughters Winnie and Theresa (born in Liverpool on 30 April 1920), and five-year-old son Richard Jnr (born in Paddington, London, on 30 October 1922), he thus spent the rest of 1927 and the first part of 1928 starring on stage in Sydney and Melbourne (where he was billed as 'The Man Who Made the Queen Laugh'), and also enjoyed success there with his musical recordings. He then, via the SS *Vancouver*, moved on to America, where, from his family's new base in California, he started the long slog on tour in vaudeville on the allied Keith-Albee and Orpheum circuits.

Described initially as 'England's Funny Man,' and later (as his accent began to drift, just a little, from Hull to Hollywood) more matter-of-factly as 'The Comedian Who Sings', he worked his way slowly but steadily up the bills, shaking off the skin of novelty that his 'foreignness' first afforded him and gradually earning recognition and respect for the quality of his comedy and his crooning.

'He has a certain clever and original way of getting his material across,' wrote one impressed critic, 'interspersing his hooey harangue with his own applause, cheers and laughter, thereby winning his audience to the point where it is about ready to eat out of his hand by curtain time.' Another enthusiastic reviewer, keen to stress his scope beyond stand-up as an all-round entertainer, judged Henderson to also be 'a fine singer' as well as 'a host in himself': 'He works smoothly, at great speed, utilises matter that is fresh here, particularly his songs, and he never misses fire.'

By 1929 his ascent was accelerating. He was playing the bigger cities, getting booked for the better venues, sharing the spotlight with such well-regarded American comics as Jack Benny, and was signed up briefly by the newly-formed RKO, and then soon after by the more established Warner Bros, with a view to grooming him for movies.

He would later claim that he was screen-tested by the producer Hal Roach with a view to pairing him (as the stout bowler-hatted man to a slender bowler-hatted man) with Stan Laurel, which, seeing as Oliver Hardy had already started working with Laurel a few months before Henderson arrived in California, seems distinctly implausible. There was certainly talk at the time of him working with Al Jolson, but that project, for some unknown reason, failed to go into production.

He did start appearing in a few minor Hollywood productions, including *The Music Shop* (1929) and *The Man from Blankley's* and *Golden Dawn* (both released in 1930). Combining his comic skills with his vocal facility, he made the most of his time in sight, with one critic judging him to be 'as distinctive in his way as Chaplin is in his'.

Such work came at just the right time, because he had lost a large portion of his and his wife's savings in the Wall Street Crash of the autumn of 1929 and he badly needed the money, but it would be the theatre, and live audiences, to which he remained most devoted. Having learned from state to state when and where to slow down his delivery and smarten up his diction, and become well aware of how to fine-tune his material for different regional and religious tastes, he now felt completely at home on the North American circuit, which was paying him what was for the time an impressive $1,000 per week.

All three of Henderson's children, with his encouragement and support, would follow him into show business. Both girls started taking dance and singing lessons (at Cansino's juvenile dancing school on Sunset and Vine, alongside Cansino's daughter, Margarita Carmen Cansino – the future Rita Hayworth), while Dickie Jnr, as he was now starting to be known, not only tagged along with his sisters, but was allowed to stand in the wings and watch his father, and other performers, rehearse and perform their routines.

It was not long before Dickie Jnr was starting to mimic some of the acts he had studied, from comic drunks to eccentric dancers, and was being used every now and then as a stooge by his father and a few of his fellow performers. He liked the more relaxed American style of stand-up – 'The Englishman leans forward to get at his audience,' he would later explain. 'The American leans back and lets his audience come to him' – and was also eager to embrace the characterful artistry of his father.

He saw his future as treading the same vaudevillian boards around America as his father had already trodden. Henderson Snr, however, would have other ideas.

Although Dick Henderson became an American citizen in 1930, signed a new movie deal with Paramount shortly after, and appeared firmly rooted to his Oakland, California, home, it would be just three years later when he decided to move with his family back to Britain.

One reason for this was that, as he fell into his forties, he had started to doubt how long he could sustain his current status as an entertainer in America. While his stand-up, although increasingly reliant on ageing material, was still proving very popular (he was now a familiar enough figure that the only bill matter he required was: 'He's Funny and He Sings'), his occasional ventures into radio and movies were being undermined by the fact that, as his son would later observe, he was quite a poor reader, and performer, of scripted material.

'Dad was brought up in a school where you have your twelve or sixteen minutes which was dynamite, and you'd honed it, and it was perfect,' Dickie told Roger Wilmut. 'But stick a script in his hand, and try to make that funny...that's why the early radio days produced stars from good readers, not funny men...his nerve went when you put a script in his hand, even though he was a better performer than the guy alongside him. He finished up doing his stage material because he was so frightened – but how many broadcasts can you do?'

That was the question that was nagging him about radio. When it came to movies, there was a further problem beyond his struggles with scripts. With the distinctiveness of his Englishness now distracting fewer movie makers, he was finding himself competing increasingly with more competent home-grown (and easier to write for) actors, such as Eugene Pallette, Edward Arnold, Edward Kennedy or Walter Connolly, for the generic 'pompous portly man' roles.

Another concern was for the future of his three children, and his son in particular. Although appreciative of Dickie's potential as a performer, and sympathetic to his impatience to start pacing the stage, he was uneasy about allowing him to immerse himself in an environment that was now striking him as unhealthily competitive and cruel.

Dickie Jnr's first break in his own fledgling show business career had come at the tender age of ten, in September 1932, when it was announced by the Fox Film Corporation that, after what was described as a long and exhaustive search (it had advertised for a boy 'of aristocratic bearing and culture,' with a 'dark, well-shaped head [and] sensitive features,' and given screen tests to 'thousands'), he had been chosen, along with three other young English children, to appear in the prestigious screen version of the Noël Coward play *Cavalcade*. Released in February of the following year, his role was that of Master Edward Marryot, the eldest of two sons by an upper-class London couple.

The movie – a sentimental slice of English social history (imagine *Downton Abbey* with more of a plot) – was hugely successful, making more than a million dollars at the box office, receiving plenty of critical praise both nationally and internationally, and winning no fewer than three Academy Awards (for Best Picture, Best Director and Best Art Direction). Dickie Jnr (who was paid $400 for his month of filming) didn't have much to do except to look depressed about Queen Victoria's death, but, with his still head and subtle expressions, he clearly took to the discipline of acting in front of a camera and was singled out for special mention by several reviewers for the 'naturalness' of his 'happily presented' performance.

As a springboard for rapid progress as a child star, he could hardly have hoped for a better vehicle, and offers of other work were starting to come in (as well as some sage insider advice – such as Spencer Tracy's thoughtful warning: 'Remember, show business is ninety per cent luck and ten per cent talent, but don't try it *without* the ten per cent'), but his father blanched at the prospect of him plunging into a professional career at such a vulnerable stage in his life. A devout Roman Catholic, Henderson Snr was also less than impressed when some of Dickie's new young friends from the studios, all of whom seemed far more precocious and cynical than him, started flirting quite aggressively with his convent-educated sisters.

For this and other reasons, therefore, Dick Henderson decided that, at the start of 1933, it was time for them all to go home. Even the intriguing news that Dickie was likely to be considered for the starring role in George Cukor's long-gestating screen adaptation of Charles Dickens's *David Copperfield* (it would be filmed the following year with Freddie Bartholomew in the part that could have been Dickie's) failed to make the father falter. They packed up their things and left on the ocean liner the RMS *Lancastria*.

Dick Henderson arrived back in England a conquering hero. Welcoming him home after almost six years away, one show business reporter wrote: 'It is very pleasing to know that one of our own comedians can, in the home of wise-cracks, stay all that time.'

The odd conservative critic seemed somewhat surprised that his satirical stories about suburban life (what he called the 'subbubs') had grown slightly saltier since he had last been on these shores – 'Dick Henderson,' tut-tutted one, 'must really dispense with the ultra-marine streak that disfigures his matter' – but most recognised that, in his usual measured way, he had simply changed to match and mirror the times.

Now advertised outside of theatres as 'Your Old Favourite,' Henderson was more popular than ever, figuring at or near to the top of the bills all over the country, mixing with fellow comic stars such as the Crazy Gang, Max Miller, Jack Hulbert, Arthur Lucan, Billy Bennett, Robb Wilton and George Robey, and also becoming one of the most in-demand and best-paid names associated with the annual pantomimes. One of the country's reliable 'cheerer-uppers' during wartime, both on stage and on radio, he would go on to appear in his second Royal Variety Performance in 1946.

He also acted as manager and chaperone to his two daughters as he arranged their entrance on to the British stage as Wyn and Triss, The Henderson Twins ('A Song, A Smile and A Dance'). Making their debut at the Argyle Theatre, Birkenhead, at the end of December 1934, they spent their first few months as performers appearing on the same bill as their doting father, before acquiring the confidence and craft to start branching out on their own.

They were signed up by one of Dick Henderson's trusted friends, the band leader and impresario Jack Hylton, who regarded them as ideal raw material that he could mould into a 'singing and swinging' British version of the all-female close harmony groups that were beginning to get big in America. Sure enough, The Henderson Twins soon became very popular, not only touring the theatres and featuring in pantomimes but also appearing regularly on radio and making the occasional record. They would continue to perform together until the middle of the Second World War, when Winnie met and married a GI named Justin McCarthy and Triss continued singing and dancing as a solo act.

Dickie Jnr, meanwhile, dutifully completed his academic education at London's 'very religious' St Joseph's College in Beulah Hill, and continued his comic education by following his father around the halls (as well as joining his sisters every now and then as a prop boy, on a fee of one pound a week, for Jack Hylton's band shows). Already bitten by the performing bug, there was little doubt now as to where his desire was driving, and all his family would do what they could to help him.

His father let him hover in the background in all the theatres he toured, allowing him to watch and learn from every kind of act that was working on each variety bill. No trick was missed, no technique left untried or untested; Dickie Jnr absorbed everything that he saw.

He would later say of these sessions: 'Every morning jugglers, acrobats, dog acts and dancers rehearsed. Always rehearsing. In exchange for dance steps from dancers, the jugglers taught dancers how to twirl a cane. Acrobats put you in a harness and taught you back-somersaults. That is why performers, then, could do a bit of everything.' That is also why, had his modesty not prevented him from adding, he, too, would grow up to be a performer who could do a bit of everything.

There remains some dispute as to when and where in Britain he made his first stage appearance as a solo performer in his own right. He would, in later years, sometimes recall the moment as being at the Birmingham Hippodrome when he was sixteen, which would have been in the autumn of 1938, or at the Middlesborough Empire earlier the same year when he filled-in for his sisters while they went off for a costume change during their spot on the touring talent show *Youth Takes a Bow*, but the records suggest that he was active, on an occasional and informal basis, at least three years before that.

One of his first theatre appearances of which we can be sure – thanks to the testimony of one of the key participants – would come at the Portsmouth

Empire in 1935, when his father, who was booked to perform there, persuaded Joe Jefferies, the venue's manager, to add the boy unofficially to the bill. Dickie did a song and a dance while his parent watched supportively from the side of the stage.

Much to his pride and delight, he went on to appear alongside Dick Snr, as father and son, in the 1935 movie *Things Are Looking Up*, a British-made musical-comedy set in and around a struggling circus, which starred Cicely Courtneidge. Playing a potential investor, the gruff cigar-chomping and tea-supping northern businessman Mr Money, and his spoilt and opinionated schoolboy son ('It all depends on the lad – if *he* likes it, *I'll* buy it'), they only shared a couple of brief scenes on the screen, but their comic rapport is quite charming, with the twelve-year-old Dickie having already picked up enough scene-stealing tricks from his forty-four-year-old father to calmly keep the focus on him even when Max Miller joins them on camera.

From 1937, the fifteen-year-old Dickie would also start appearing more regularly, as a solo act, on the same bills as his father, as 'Dick Henderson Jnr: A Song, A Joke, A Dance'. Like Dick Snr, he was not a tall man, but, unlike him, he was skinny and athletic, blessed with much better looks, a warm and slightly husky voice and with a stage persona that was, by comparison, still intriguingly inchoate.

Dick Snr would continue to watch his son from the wings whenever possible, dispensing hard-earned wisdom along the way. 'If you want to get a laugh with a joke,' he would say, 'you've got to go up vocally at the end, and if you move your arms up, your voice will automatically go up, too.' Then there was his warning about milking the applause too much after each gag: 'Don't get too much applause during your act, because you won't get as much at the end.' He also warned against taking multiple bows at the completion of a well-received performance: 'You don't want to do that. Take one; one good one is better than five, running on and off.'

He was also by no means disinclined to be cruel to be kind. During one of these early outings, for example, he saw his son struggle to win over a docile crowd, eventually resorting, out of a mounting sense of panic, to parroting the kind of cliches (e.g. 'I know you're out there – I can hear you breathing') that he had heard so many struggling comics bark out bitterly in the past. Eventually, feeling utterly defeated, he slouched off the stage and straight into a slap from his waiting father.

'What was *that* for?' gasped the startled young performer. 'That,' snapped Dick Snr, 'was for *telling* them you were dying a death! If you hadn't come out with all that crap, they'd have been none the wiser. They didn't *know* you were dying a death until you *told* them – *they* thought you were *always* that bad!'

'It was a lesson,' Dickie would later say, 'I never forgot.' There would be many more of them, too.

He went on to win praise for his spirited performance as Simple Simon in the 1939/40 production of the pantomime *Red Riding Hood* at the Town Hall, Pontypridd, shone again the following year (alongside his father and sisters) in a long-running touring revue called *Business as Usual*, and then had an educational experience during a week with his father at the Tivoli Theatre in Scunthorpe as the support acts for the so-called 'Queen of Striptease' Phyllis Dixey.

In 1942, just as he was about to appear in his first West End production – *Sky High*, starring Hermione Gingold, Hermione Baddeley and Naunton Wayne, at the Phoenix Theatre – Dickie Henderson was called up, at the age of nineteen, to serve in the Army. For the next three years, although frustrated by the fact that his fledgling career had stalled, he would have, by his own admission, 'an extremely cushy war': rising to the rank of Second Lieutenant, he did not leave Britain and saw no action.

Once demobbed in 1946, and now in his mid-twenties, he raced to resume his show business momentum. Singing, dancing, performing comedy skits and essaying some Hollywood impressions, he toured in a Ralph Reader revue entitled *Something to Shout About* (a title, he would later claim, that proved more than somewhat misleading, although the show did run for eighteen months); stationed himself in a succession of summer seasons (most notably Cecil G. Buckingham's slapstick revue *Seaside Showboat* at Ramsgate's Royal Victoria Pavilion in 1949, for which he received exceptional praise and attracted plenty of interest from influential London promoters); appeared in a pantomime (*The King and Queen of Hearts*) at the Brighton Hippodrome with the popular northern double-act of Jewel and Warriss; made his cabaret debut at the Coconut Grove in Regent Street; made his West End debut at the Savoy Theatre in the Alan Melville revue *A La Carte* (where one critic judged him 'a versatile artist on distinctive lines that owe nothing to the parental tradition'); and, at the end of the decade, won a role in the glamorous *Folies Bergère* show at the London Hippodrome.

He also met and fell in love with the Texas-born singer and dancer Dixie Jewell Ross (one of the Ross Sisters trio), whom he married in the summer of 1948 (on 13 June) at Westminster Cathedral. They would go on to have a son (Matthew) and a daughter (Linda) together.

A significant change in his act came the following year, after receiving some helpful advice from one of The Marx Brothers, whom he was supporting during their sixteen-week tour of Britain. Chico Marx, after seeing Dickie perform a few times, took him to one side and told him: 'You've got to change your material. Some of it's too raw.'

The older performer had noticed that, whenever anxious, Henderson had resorted to 'blue material' in the hope of getting more laughs. Chico explained that not only was this lazy, it was also, for a fresh-faced twenty-seven-year-old comic, fairly ineffective, because such 'worldly' gags simply did not ring true.

The old vaudevillian urged him to only use material that specifically applied to him and his own experiences, so that it was not only more believable but would also be harder for other comics to steal. Henderson took the advice to heart, developing his own material, and seeking more from his writer friends, and adding it to his act. From this point on, thanks in part to Chico Marx, Dickie Henderson would be a more distinctive, and more authentic, comic performer, and it won him much-improved reviews.

By the start of the 1950s, reports of his stage act were noting that it was eliciting his 'usual ovation', and there was widespread praise for his versatility. He appeared in the West End alongside Diana Dors and Naunton Wayne in a comedy murder mystery called *Remains to Be Seen* (1952), and would do so again as the wily local interpreter Sakini (the role later played in the movie version by Marlon Brando) in *The Teahouse of the August Moon* (1955-6); started a recording career; performed cabaret in the US as well as the UK; and contributed some one-off stand-up spots to the BBC's *Workers' Playtime*. Hailed as someone who was 'fast becoming one of our foremost performers,' he was beginning to overtake his father in terms both of the size of the venue and the fee received.

Among the familiar features of his act at this stage were his comedy typologies. These observational pieces had been an element of his stage repertoire since he was a teenager – e.g. 'The ways in which audience members laugh in different parts of a theatre'; 'How diverse people speak on the telephone'; 'How different characters behave in ballroom dancing'; 'How different classes act when drunk' – and the format was now used to explore such topical themes as the generation gap and social mobility. Much quoted in newspaper reviews, these funny and fecund routines would prove enduringly influential, as the likes of *The Frost Report's* 1966 'Class Sketch' ('I know my place...') implicitly confirmed.

Another ingredient, reliant on years of experience, was his gift for eccentric dancing ('dance doodling,' as the author John Fisher would call it). This was a technical skill that he had started assimilating during his youth in America, watching such legomanic specialists as Joe Bennett, Ray Bolger, Eddie Foy Snr and Joe Frisco, as well as his father's friends and colleagues from the British stage, such as Wilson, Keppel and Betty and Max Wall. He ended up mastering the art so well that, besides being able to imitate all of his predecessors' distinctive styles with remarkable accuracy, he also stamped his own signature on the skill, and, again, inspired a mini revival in the speciality.

Then there were his various physical comedy routines, most of which featured Bergsonian battles with inanimate objects, such as doors, hats, bottles, soda siphons and whatever happened to be the latest gadgets. Probably the most memorable – and much copied – of these was the microphone routine, a very flexible and multi-faceted sequence which saw him, depending on the mood and situation, either having to keep tugging at the trailing cord as he tried to croon a tune (an idea quickly assimilated by an impressed Norman Wisdom) or struggle with a connection that kept cutting out (a concept that he and Norman Collier appeared to have developed independently of each other at roughly the same time), or numerous other technical tussles and malfunctions.

He also excelled at a musical-comedy routine that saw him play a drunk, perched on a bar stool, spilling drink on himself and burning his fingers with a cigarette while he attempted in vain to sing the Harold Arlen/Johnny Mercer hit, 'One for My Baby,' just like Frank Sinatra. This developed into such a virtuoso performance that audiences would still be requesting it for decades after it first won praise.

The interest in him was considerable. Already billed, somewhat generously, as 'Radio's Brightest Personality' (he had not actually been on that many broadcasts so far), and attracting more than a few influential fans in the Press (with one of them responding well to the fact that he was not just 'a pleasing young character who dances and sings,' but was also a comedian who 'sails a little close to the wind in his anecdotes'), several producers were pondering plans to move him on to better things.

His big break as an adult performer arrived in March 1953, when one of his father's old friends, Arthur Askey, chose him to be a regular in his new BBC TV show, *Before Your Very Eyes*. The exposure it afforded him, back in those one-channel days, was immense, giving him nationwide fame more or less overnight.

He also, in the process, became a lifelong friend of Askey, a performer for whom he would have the greatest affection and respect, while Askey would come to regard Dickie as the son he never had. Marvelling in particular at the older comic's ability to think on his feet no matter what pressure he might have been under, Dickie studied him carefully while trying hard not to laugh at all of his rapid and unerringly funny ad-libs (which would continue to flow right up to late on in his life, such as the time when Askey, upon hearing from Henderson that the Tudor ship the *Mary Rose* had finally been raised from the sea bed, exclaimed without missing a beat: 'Oh, good, some of my band parts are on it').

Henderson's own versatility, even in those days, was starting to be discussed by a few as if it was some kind of problem – 'With so many strings to his bow,' one critic commented, 'it must be difficult for Dickie to decide what comes next' – but a more common reaction was one of admiration as the star now dubbed 'Debonaire Dickie' moved with such assurance from one genre to the next. Impresarios such as Val Parnell were especially impressed by the breadth of his talents, along with the urbane unflappability of his demeanour, prompting them to start regarding him as an ideal 'safe pair of hands' to host and hold together their high-profile variety spectaculars.

It would be Parnell (the managing director of ATV) who relied on him the most during the next few years, hiring him initially as the compere of his *Sunday Night at the London Palladium* show in 1956, and then, either directly or via his various directors, offering him first choice on innumerable other major shows in the years that followed.

There was a moment, however, when it looked as though Parnell was set to be Henderson's nemesis. A man with the power (and temperament) to make or break artists' careers, he clashed with the young performer very early on in their relationship and, as a consequence, could easily have dropped him (and blocked him) for good.

It happened in 1956, when Henderson, fresh from a summer tour of America (where he appeared in an episode of the hit Jeannie Carson sitcom *Hey, Jeannie!*), was offered a new TV series, co-starring with the wonderfully droll Scottish comedian, Chic Murray, and Murray's wife, Maidie. Entitled *Young and Foolish*, and billed as 'song, fun and dance show,' it was going to be produced by Dicky Leeman, and written (primarily) by Michael Bentine and Marty Feldman.

The writers and performers met each other for the first time on the Monday before the first live transmission the following Saturday. It did not go well. Personalities clashed, arguments broke out and the session dissolved into acrimony.

There was no major problem between the two stars. Henderson considered Murray 'a very funny man', and the Scotsman, in turn, found the Englishman urbane and engaging. The main problem concerned the scripts. Neither Feldman nor Bentine seemed sure of what they should, and could, be writing, the two comedians were both suggesting their own ideas, and none of them seemed to be agreeing with any of the others about anything.

Chic Murray, eager for the exposure on English screens, was inclined to carry on despite agreeing broadly with his co-star's complaint that the material was woefully sub-standard and tonally erratic. Henderson, however, was so unhappy with the situation that, after working on the first show, he asked to be released from his contract 'on the grounds that the public should enjoy a little respect'.

The series, as a result, limped ahead with Henderson's presence promised in the previews, but with his absence evident on the screen, and the show was abandoned after just three editions. It was a blow to Chic Murray, whose undeserved bad luck would continue later that year when he (along with, ironically enough, Dickie Henderson) was selected to appear in the Royal Variety Performance at the London Palladium, only for it to be cancelled at the last minute because of an escalation of the Suez Crisis.

It also seemed to be a serious blow for Dickie. Parnell, furious at the Henderson-sized hole in his schedules, blamed Dickie for the debacle and told him in no uncertain terms that he would not be welcome on future ATV productions.

This unofficial boycott would, as it happened, be challenged as early as the start of 1957, when the talented young producer Brian Tesler, on his first day at ATV after being poached by Parnell from the BBC, informed his new bosses that he wanted for his initial project to make a Saturday night show with Dickie Henderson as its star. Parnell, sure enough, moved to veto the proposal, but Tesler had a clause in his brand-new contract that allowed him the power to cast his own programmes.

Frustrated, Parnell had no option but to allow the 'difficult' performer an unexpectedly swift return to ATV, but, still determined to register his displeasure, he insisted that the name of the show would have to be *Val Parnell's Saturday Spectacular* and not, as Tesler had intended, *The Dickie Henderson Show*.

The opening edition, however, proved so popular, with Henderson's performance so impressive, that even Parnell felt obliged to back down. He sent Tesler a congratulatory telegram, which read: 'Terrific. It can now be called *The Dickie Henderson Show*'. The series continued to win warm reviews, and its star – now that he was recognised as its star – was able to relax and start to enjoy himself on screen (especially when the show very memorably reunited him with his father for the 10th August edition).

Fortunately for Henderson, the ATV impresario's ire soon abated, and, after some diplomatic exchanges, the promising performer was taken firmly back into the fold. Indeed, a sign of how quickly this froideur had thawed came later that year, when Parnell awarded him (thirty-one years after Dick Henderson Snr had received the same honour) the first of what would turn out in total to be his six prestigious appearances on the *Royal Variety Performance*.

This was followed by the programme that was arguably the peak – or at least the beginning of the peak – of his career: *The Dickie Henderson Half-Hour*. Overseen, on this occasion, by the old friend of the family Jack Hylton, it was made by Associated-Rediffusion for the ITV network, would run for two series, from 1958 to 1959, and established Henderson, beyond any doubt, as one of Britain's premier entertainers of the era.

Among its regular features were stand-up spots, songs and dances, the odd movie or TV spoof, and, in a knowing nod to the observational approach of Dick Snr, there were mini sitcom-style sketches 'based on the idea of how the average person might meet [the] everyday problems of life'. He was supported on the show by Anthea Askey (the daughter of Arthur), Eve Lister, Bernard Hunter and Eric Delaney, along with a succession of special guests, and his rapport with Askey, in particular, became one of the highlights of the show.

What was most notable in all these elements was how unusually rounded Dickie Henderson's range of technical talents was. It did not matter what he did – slapstick, sophisticated dialogue, gag-driven sequences, character-driven sequences, routines that relied on energy and movement and ones that required subtlety and stillness – he did it all with remarkable precision and style.

However, what let him down on these shows was the quality of the scripts, which were actually, at least in part, adapted by Jimmy Grafton (Henderson's regular writer) and others from US TV's Sid Caesar vehicle *Your Show of Shows*. This was actually a fairly common practice among Britain's commercial TV companies of the time (the best of the homegrown writers, now protected by their own agencies, were getting increasingly expensive), and it was an especially enthusiastic policy of Jack Hylton's, who had already bulk-bought enough foreign material to feed most of the needs of his channel for several years. It was also not the most foolish of moves if one judged it on the principle that 'if you have to steal then steal from the best' – Caesar's large team of writers included Mel Brooks, Neil Simon and Carl Reiner.

In this particular case, however, it was a poorly executed policy, with little effort expended into updating and revising the material for Henderson and his guests. Although the star was allowed to add some of his own tried and tested stage routines, he was expected to move ahead equipped mainly with nothing more than second-hand material.

It was a strangely careless way for the producers to treat a star whom they genuinely valued, because he could easily have been left drained by the strain it put on him. Unlike, say, Tony Hancock, whose own personality was being promoted by the most sensitively bespoke scripts every week, Henderson was having to impose his personality on to routines that had been designed – very carefully indeed – for someone else entirely.

Several of the critics not only hated the practice but also made a point of complaining in print about it. 'It's all old Sid Caesar material re-jigged for Mr Henderson,' one of them exclaimed. 'We might as well hand over the whole works to American TV,' grumbled another. 'These tattered pages,' moaned a third about the American hand-me-downs, 'are then thrown on to our TV screens without even a shred of adaptation being done to them.'

Henderson himself was quoted as saying that he would have much preferred to be using original, tailor-made scripts, but, showing loyalty to Hylton, claimed that it was not currently financially sustainable to restrict a British writer like Jimmy Grafton to working full-time on one single project. 'If I kept Jimmy to myself,' he said, 'I would need to pay him three to four hundred pounds a week to make up the loss of other markets'.

The show, in spite of these regular carps by the critics, still easily made the top ten most-watched shows on a regular basis (earning an impressive 70 Nielsen Network Rating), thanks to Henderson's energy, ingenuity and expertise in finding new ways to cover the cracks in the comedy and lift the material up to a higher level. Another sign of its – and his – success was the fact that during September 1958, in between the first and second series, Henderson received, but turned down, an offer from the BBC to make a similar show for them (which would have earned him £700 – a sizeable sum at the time by the standards of the BBC – for each of the proposed thirteen episodes).

The second series fared about the same as the first: there were still a few less-than-fulsome reviews (although Bryan Michie, the well-known producer, put into print his praise for what he considered the show's 'marvellous use' of its recycled American material), but the audience figures remained strong and Henderson's own popularity continued to soar. The only setback that he would suffer during this otherwise positive period was the sudden loss of his father.

Dick Snr died, aged sixty-seven, on 15th October 1958 – three days after he heard the news that he had been chosen to appear in what would have been his third Royal Variety Performance on the 3rd of November. Dogged for a number of years by diabetes, and depressed by the closing of so many of the old halls he used to grace, he had confided to his family that he would probably bow out of the business after his forthcoming appearance in the presence of royalty.

Described by his fellow residents in Chelsea as 'a kind and happy man' who 'never complained about anything' and was popular 'among men of all classes,' it was added that his son's own recent successes had given him 'a real deep feeling of pride and satisfaction'. Asked about his attitude in his final few years, one neighbour said: 'He reckoned that he had a full life and enjoyed every moment of it.'

'What he did not tell us about certain aspects of mothers-in-law, sweethearts, marriage, and a score more familiars of everyday life, was probably not worth hearing,' wrote one critic in tribute. 'His range may have been limited but it went to the very heart and spirit of the matter; and the matter was concerned with the ironical side of the life he brought before us so vividly.'

A fixture in the show business firmament for more than forty years, his loss was felt widely, but, of course, by none as much as his son. Dick Snr had remained his mentor, unofficial manager and main cheerleader throughout his career, and the memory of his creative presence would stay, as an unmistakeable shadow, on every stage that Dickie stepped.

Dickie's own career now went on from strength to strength. He had a standing invitation to appear on *The Ed Sullivan Show* whenever he was in America (where his style and reliability were warmly admired, with one critic going so far as to claim that he was 'the greatest British performer to play [there] since Noël Coward'); returned to the West End stage in another musical-comedy, *When in Rome* (1959); released numerous singles; hosted a quiz show called *For Love or Money* and acted alongside Brian Rix in the first television version of *Doctor in the House* (both 1960); and starred in countless BBC radio programmes, including his own edition of *Desert Island Discs* (again in 1960).

What he would most have wanted to do at this stage, had a good enough opportunity presented itself, was to move (back) into movies, but the right kind of vehicle never came. 'One of my idols,' he would later say, 'is Jack Lemmon, and all the parts he played were the parts I wanted to play, but they didn't make those types of movie over here.'

Frustrated in his efforts to break onto the big screen, he turned back to the small one and started his own sitcom, *The Dickie Henderson Show*, for Foster TV productions/Associated-Rediffusion at the start of the new decade. Modelled quite blatantly, once again, on US star vehicles of the period such as *I Love Lucy* and *The Red Buttons Show* (but anticipating the very similar *The Dick Van Dyke Show*, which would reach the screen just under a year later), it featured Henderson as a comic version of himself, June Laverick as his wife, John Parsons as their young son and the Canadian-born Lionel Murton (one of British TV's all-purpose North Americans) as his musical manager and best friend, Jack.

Co-written by Jimmy Grafton and Jeremy Lloyd (with a fair amount of support, as usual, from second-hand sources), it aimed unashamedly to cosily entertain a broad middle-class mainstream audience ('I'm a happy family man, yes sir,' sang Dickie at the start of each episode. 'Love my wife, I do what I can for her'), and it succeeded. The chemistry between Henderson and June Laverick – and her later replacement, from 1967 onwards, Isla Blair – was excellent (he always worked well with women), and the kind of domestic and romantic subjects covered elicited easy identification from a family audience.

It was also the kind of show that exuded an upbeat atmosphere – not just because of the feel-good storylines but also because the performers seemed to be genuinely having fun. Re-takes were rather more common than usual due to the tendency of guest performers, especially, to 'corpse' when working with the always inventive Henderson, and there were innumerable occasions when giggling or smirking faces had to be half-hidden from the cameras to get through a scene unedited.

Pete Murray, for example, would recall his own struggles when he appeared in one episode: 'It was an extremely funny show, so funny that Dickie and

I would be convulsed with laughter at all the rehearsals, even the camera rehearsal. Came the actual transmission: "Don't worry, Pete," drawled Dickie, "I have never laughed on a show in all my years in show business." Famous last words. We had got through two-thirds of the show, avoiding each other's gaze as much as possible, and I was drinking tea out of the saucer and burping. Dickie's eyes glazed over and, quite uncharacteristically, he fluffed a line – instead of "TV" he said "twee". That did it: the saucer of tea went, I went, the camera crew went – and the audience went.'

The show was, in short, one of the most reliable, if undemanding, family-orientated sitcoms of its time. Beginning on ITV on 14th November 1960, it ran for a total of nine series (comprising no fewer than one-hundred-and-sixteen episodes) over the course of the next eight years, thus ensuring that Henderson remained one of the most familiar figures on British television during one of the most celebrated eras in its history.

There would be another reason, however, for his prominence and popularity, and that was his many appearances through all these years as a much-admired master of ceremonies. No other performer was appreciated, and trusted, more in that demanding role than Dickie Henderson.

Bruce Forsyth, of course, came close, but, being the force of nature that he was, he had a habit of taking over the shows he hosted, which could be a positive thing when the guests were uninspiring, but would sometimes seem unnecessarily distracting when other stars craved their own time and space in which to shine. Henderson, in contrast, was a more flexible kind of compere, able and willing to step back as well as forward depending on the needs of any mood or moment.

With his transatlantic tan and twang he was particularly assured when presiding over an international cast. Known to most of the performers thanks to his own many tours abroad, he was able to provide a strong and satisfying link between them all, from up-and-coming London comics to seasoned American crooners, from South African ballerinas to Italian hand puppets, all while subtly choreographing the British audience's reactions to the more unfamiliar and exotic of the acts.

Arguably one of his defining contributions as a compere came on the evening of 4th November 1963, when, in the presence of The Queen Mother and Princess Margaret, he had to maintain order, pacing, an upbeat atmosphere and a smooth sense of cohesion during a three-hour-long Royal Variety Performance that featured such disparate figures as Marlene Dietrich, the stars of *Steptoe and Son*, Flanders and Swann, Charlie Drake,

Nadia Nerina with the cast of *Sleeping Beauty*, Max Bygraves, the puppets Pinky and Perky, Buddy Greco, Harry Secombe and the cast of *Pickwick*, Luis Alberto del Parana and Los Paraguayos, The Clark Brothers and The Beatles.

This kind of stardust-sprinkled smorgasbord of a spectacular would have proved a challenge at any 'ordinary' time for a solitary host, but on this particular occasion it was made doubly difficult by the fact that central to this event were The Beatles at the very moment when their popularity was racing through unprecedented levels of intensity. The media interest in the show, as a consequence, was exceptionally strong, as was the police presence outside the Prince of Wales Theatre as the screaming crowds of fans were kept, more or less, under control.

After the group had run through their set, and John Lennon had made his instantly infamous suggestion about the posh people rattling their jewels while the common ones clapped their hands, there was a palpable sense of relief on the face of the show's organiser, Bernard Delfont, at the realisation first that, contrary to his sceptical expectations, the band had not died a death in front of such an upmarket middle-class audience, and, second, that it was going to be Dickie Henderson (whom he considered 'a tower of strength') who had the unenviable task of following 'that'.

The host, well aware of the extraordinary impact the band had just had, but mindful of the need to move things forward, strolled on and handled things with his usual good grace. 'The Beatles,' he declared with a suave smile. 'Aren't they fabulous? So successful...So young...Frightening!'

It was an appropriately calm response, but also quite a considered one. No one was more attuned to the first hints of seismic shifts in show business than Dickie Henderson. He knew, right then, what many of his contemporaries would start to realise in the days and weeks that would follow: that a new generation, a new mood and a new means was coming to the fore, and that he, like most of the others backstage, would soon have to navigate their way through a very different landscape.

He adapted as smoothly as many expected. Still devoted to entertaining the broadest of audiences, he continued doing what he did best, where he knew it would work best, and with a classiness that commanded respect.

He stayed active on both sides of the Atlantic, flying over fairly frequently each year to work in America (aside from his countless appearances in theatres and night clubs, and run of six-week residencies at the Riviera Hotel in Las Vegas, he was also a guest on both the Jack Paar and Johnny Carson incarnations of *The Tonight Show*) as well as Australia and a number of other countries. Throughout the Sixties and Seventies, he remained for many in the entertainment world the epitome of professional excellence.

He also continued to be one of the most popular performers among his peers in the industry. Roy Hudd, for example, would describe him as 'perhaps the most versatile and certainly the smoothest, most laid-back comedian it had been my pleasure to see,' adding that 'he danced, sang and delivered one-liners wonderfully, and even his prat-falls were, somehow, classy...He was, without doubt, the best I ever saw'.

Eric Sykes would agree, counting Henderson among his own comedy heroes. Describing him as 'the most unassuming person I ever met,' he regarded him, nonetheless, as 'a person who would be successful in whatever profession or calling he put his mind to'. Marvelling at his remarkable mix of abilities in particular, Sykes reflected that 'it wouldn't surprise me if he could ride a unicycle whilst juggling a set of Encyclopaedia Brittanicas and at the same time whistling the "Marseillaise".'

Eric Morecambe was another great admirer. He enjoyed Henderson's address at the memorial service for Arthur Askey so much that he wrote to him the next day, 'booking' him for when his own funeral happened. 'I'll pay you,' he added, 'when I see you down there.'

A reason why such respect was also accompanied by so much affection was the fact that Henderson – 'a gentleman in every sense,' said Sykes – was known to be so freely supportive of any of his fellow performers. Educated by his father from an early age about the old adage 'be kind to everyone on the way up, because you'll meet the same people on the way down,' he always behaved in such a way, even though no such descent would ever happen, and became, especially in his later years, an invaluable source of advice and encouragement to anyone with whom he worked, passing on the tricks of the trade to countless performers ranging from Bill Owen to Eddie Large, and from stand-ups and sketch artists to dancers and West End singers.

He was also the kind of star who retained a healthy degree of irreverence for his own exalted status and delighted in telling stories against himself. One example concerns the time that he, as a proud half-Scouser, agreed to take part in a benefit show at the Liverpool Empire for one of the city's most decorated and admired footballers, Ian Callaghan. Henderson had to drive straight back to London after the performance was over, leaving the host Jimmy Tarbuck and the rest of the participating artists to enjoy the post-show champagne reception.

'Hey, Jimmy,' shouted one very large and merry Scouser, 'I've never seen Henderson *live* before, and I must say he has tremendous class, and fantastic material. He's suave, smooth, sophisticated, in fact a superb performer. But on television – he's like you.' 'What's that?' replied an intrigued Tarbuck. And the answer came back: 'CRAP!'

Henderson was too much a product of his profession to show any private sadness, but there had been some crises behind the scenes. Apart from the loss of his father, there was also the tragically premature death, at the age of thirty-three, of his wife, Dixie, on 10th July 1963.

She had been at their home in Abbotsbury Road, Holland Park, in Kensington, when their daily help arrived that morning. A note on her bedroom door had read: 'Please don't disturb. I'm taking drugs for a heavy cold,' but then a noise was heard and she was found unconscious on the floor. She later died at a nearby hospital.

Dickie, upon hearing the news of the initial discovery, had cancelled that night's performance in his Brighton summer show and hurried back to London. 'I was too late,' the distraught star would tell reporters. 'Dixie was my life.'

According to the subsequent coroner's report, she had taken fifteen or sixteen barbiturate sleeping pills. An open verdict was reached as to whether she had deliberately taken her own life or merely attempted a cry for help, but it was noted that it had been on her and Dickie's fifteenth wedding anniversary.

Dickie (who said that he would live with the guilt for the rest of his days) would later acknowledge that he and Dixie had been undergoing a trial separation at the time, and he had not seen her for the previous two weeks while he was performing on the East Sussex coast, but added that he was actually soon due to return home to discuss a reconciliation. He noted that, although she had been feeling aimless and depressed in the past year or so, and somewhat resentful of the many other people who were laying claim to his time and attention, he had invested recently in a fashion shop for her in Park Lane, and her spirits had seemed to be lifting.

Described as 'inconsolable' by his old friend and near-neighbour Jimmy Jewel, he struggled to work for a while after suffering such a loss, and, as he later reflected, audiences struggled to know how to react to him back on stage. They knew, he said, 'what I was going through and could not understand how I could try to be funny,' and, although they gave him overwhelmingly warm ovations, 'the laughs were not the same'.

It would take a while for both parties to return to an outlook that felt 'normal'. Dickie went through the motions, fulfilling his many engagements, while relying on a circle of close show business friends for emotional support.

He struggled on as a single parent to his two children until a couple of years later, when he became involved with a twenty-seven-year-old assistant TV producer named Gwyneth Wycherley. They married, very quietly, on 6th July 1965, and Dickie, while striving to find more time for his family, continued working much as before, staying as busy as ever as one decade gave way to the next.

He was more selective than before as far as his British appearances were concerned (although he was one of the 'special guest stars' whom all of his colleagues craved), but elsewhere he became, if anything, even more active. There were tours of Europe, Australia, New Zealand, South Africa, Hong Kong and North and South America, and some high-profile cabaret engagements in Las Vegas and Los Angeles, where he would be welcomed back as a friend and peer by the likes of Bob Hope, George Burns, Phil Silvers and Johnny Carson. He was also a tireless campaigner for and supporter of countless charities, both national and international, raising fortunes for their upkeep and their various other needs and initiatives.

If there was one criticism some of his admirers might have directed towards him during these days, it concerned the fact that, while his industry remained stable, his ambition seemed to decline. The inclination, for a while at least, was to coast.

'I think that if his friends had any professional regret about Dickie,' Brian Tesler would tell Peter Cotes for his tribute in *Sincerely Dickie: A Dickie Henderson Collection*, 'it was that, having reached [a certain level], perhaps he could have worked harder at commissioning new material. The material he used was the same for years; he reached that peak and stayed there.'

Probably the most memorable of his later projects, at least as far as domestic television appearances are concerned, were the three hour-long specials that he made alongside Bob Monkhouse for ITV, spread out over 1977 and 1978, called *I'm Bob, He's Dickie*. The brainchild of Francis Essex, the Director of Production at ATV, it was the sort of pairing that seemed not only apt but also somewhat risk-laden, seeing as both entertainers (who had been friends for many years) had long been obliged to struggle against the unfair perception that, for all their talent, there was an off-putting air of unctuousness about them. Their union could therefore have triggered a turn-off twice over among some sections of the audience, if it had not been for the fact that both of them were so keen to seize on the chance to prove their critics wrong.

They succeeded. It was, predictably, a stylish set of shows, rich in their mix of crosstalk, sketches, songs and dances, and it certainly confirmed, amongst other things, what a consummate all-rounder Dickie Henderson continued to be.

His comic timing, for example, was not just immaculate but was also – even more of a rarity – executed in a believably natural manner (DICKIE: 'Have a drink.' BOB: 'I have planned this show as an evening of bunting and frolics.' DICKIE: 'Don't have a drink').

His acrobatic skills, as a man in his mid-fifties, were as sound as ever. There were backward falls, slips, slides and tumbles, all executed with seemingly effortless flair.

His dancing ability, and versatility, was demonstrated in several routines, including one in which he switched smoothly from one style and tempo to another with elegant poise and precision. There were also some finely-judged sitcom-like scenes with the likes of Sylvia Syms, several effective impressions, and a brief reprise of his much-loved 'drunk on a bar-stool' business. There was even one moment, thanks to a particularly pertinent piece of trick photography, when he had a song and dance routine ('I'm Dickie – He's Dickie') in which he collaborated with himself.

Whatever he did on these shows, he did with an engaging warmth, wit and energy. It was like a series of masterclasses in how to perform each activity properly, personably and professionally.

He followed these double act productions with a couple of similar specials of his own, *I'm Dickie – That's Show Business*, which further demonstrated his myriad talents. Simultaneously a singular performance and also a curation of a whole era in multi-media entertainment, there was something precious, in the best sense, about these programmes, as it was clear not only that he was one of the few genuine all-round entertainers left, but also that no one would, or could, follow in his footsteps.

Dickie Henderson died at his home in Essex, from pancreatic cancer, on 22nd September 1985, at the age of sixty-two. Awarded the OBE in 1977, his career had lasted more than half a century, and he had remained busy and in-demand right up to the end.

There were many tributes in the days that followed. They all stressed his kindness, his versatility and his exceptional command of every aspect of show business technique.

'He saw the good in people and didn't dwell on something that couldn't be changed,' said his daughter, Linda. 'From what I am told he was a good friend. He was most certainly a good friend to his children.'

'He was firm but fair to everybody,' said his son, Matthew. 'He was his own man, but his respect was for anybody who showed himself in his eyes to be a *professional* wherever he found him or her, in any field of human endeavour.'

His former producer Brian Tesler hailed his 'all-rounder' ability and his unfailing decency. 'He was immensely loyal to his friends,' he said, 'even when he knew it did him no particular good professionally.'

The actor Anton Rodgers would say of him that 'underneath all that skill and perfectionism was the rare ingredient – charm. He had it in abundance, and it was effortless – like all real charmers'.

Sir John Mills made a similar observation: 'His art concealed his art – it was so relaxed and easy. Yet what he did was far from easy – it was the result of years of sheer hard work, learning his craft and then refining it. It was work, it was pleasure, it was *style*.'

Sir Anthony Quayle admired his attitude: 'He never played down to his audience: always up. His unique skill was to share with them an amused, ironic friendship in the hazards and indignities of modern life.' He added: 'But it was as a friend that he meant most to me. He was the best company in the world that to be sure – but he was much more: he knew where he stood in life, and that helped his friends to put the world in perspective.'

Pete Murray celebrated his professionalism: 'I have appeared with many comics but nobody like Dickie. Totally unselfish – all he demanded was a hundred per cent effort from his team – and he got it.'

Eric Sykes, who described him as 'one of the greats,' spoke of how 'privileged' he felt to 'have been one of his friends'.

Jimmy Tarbuck, who had been one of the last people to see him alive, spoke of his inextinguishable sense of humour. 'A nurse had said, "You look much better today". And he had replied, "That shows you how bad I was yesterday".'

One newspaper, noting his 'tireless' charity work, simply called him 'the little man with a big heart'.

'When I go,' he had said, 'I hope people will say, "He's a pro, he knew what it was all about".' It would be apt, too, if people now really appreciate what it really meant, and what it really took, for him to be a pro. There was nothing shallow about his slickness; there was nothing dubious about his dexterity.

Dickie Henderson could not help his heritage. He could not help the fact that a beaming Cary Grant would seek him out to reminisce about the comic art of his father, or that Mickey Rooney would happily swap stories with him about the Hollywood of the Thirties, or that Sammy Davis Jr would ask him for insights as to how to perfect the 'flash dancing' that Henderson had picked up as a boy from the Nicholas Brothers. It was all part of the elaborate fabric of his life. He simply had seen, heard and learned more than most of those who now tried to amuse and entertain.

In a country and a culture that, traditionally, has always been more comfortable with amateurism rather than professionalism, Dickie Henderson's 'classiness' may have been seen by the more cynical as a carapace behind which a more Corinthian, and less calculating, soul was left to languish, but that was a view that mistook a craft that came from rich and wide experience for a cravenness borne of commercialism. Dickie Henderson was 'classy' and 'polished' and 'professional' because he was good enough, and intelligent enough, and responsible enough to know when and why it was actually needed.

If a show required an orderly context within which another comic could be chaotic, he would supply it. If a one-off special needed a sense of glossy coherence to contain the otherwise messy disparateness of its other guests, he could provide it.

There was, however, far more to him than this, and the fact that it tended, in later years, to be under-used by some was more the fault of the producers than it ever was his own. Protean talents are either showcased to saturation or straitjacketed into singularity. Dickie Henderson's fate, far too often, was the latter, but whatever filter through which he was forced from one show to the next, some or other of his rare and special gifts would always shine through.

It was said, during his prime, that he owed his success to 'an old-fashioned gimmick called talent'. If that seemed something worth celebrating at the time, it seems even more worth celebrating today.

GUIDE FORMAT

The layout of the listings may seem a little daunting at first, but trying to pack this much information into a book does necessitate some compromises over instant readability. Each listing is split into up to four levels of information, though most use three or fewer. The first of these levels reflects the information that relates to the programme as a whole. Now this 'programme' might be a one-off play, a six-part series, a serial with over 3,000 episodes (though that is a bit unlikely in a book that mainly features light entertainment) or anything in between. Details which remain constant throughout the whole of the programme's run will be listed here. In most cases this means that the companies which commissioned and made the programme will be listed here, as would any writer, director or producer who fulfilled that role for the every episode. The duration, in minutes, will be generally found here too, as will the name of the company whose broadcast dates are used in the episode section. Here's a fictitious sample entry:

THE COBBLER'S LAST
Produced by BBC Birmingham for BBC1. Transmission details are for BBC1.
Usual running length: 50 minutes.

Programme credit(s):   Music by Alison Crosley; executive producer Lenny Leonard.
Programme performer(s):   Peter Templeton (Hugh Rogers); Jill Dawson (Phillippa Maitland); Rob Cosworth (Phil Mulraney).

Where a programme is split into more than one series, the next entry will be for the first series. This may be no more than a simple entry saying just "SERIES 1", but it can contain the same types of information as found at programme level. For example:

SERIES 1
Season credit(s): Produced by Toni Simmonds.

In this case, no single producer worked throughout the various series of *The Cobbler's Last* but Toni Simmonds fulfilled this role on the first series, so she gets credited here. Someone else will no doubt be credited for the second and third series. In most cases, the next set of entries will be the episodes. Here are more equally fictional examples:

Holding / Source Format

16.10.1967 **The First Last**   R1N|n / 40
Written by Healey Smith; directed by Charles Black.
Annalisé Moore (Juanita), Adrian Oz (Mr Jenkins), Michael Scruple (Horace), Jacob Worthy (Maurice), Michael Bridewell (Boris), James Bullock (Dorrice).

23.10.1967 **Last – but not Least**   J / Live
Written by Jackson Robb; directed by Charles Black.
Alan Hurley (Collier), Lucy Hepple (Cooper), Keith Appletree (Saddler), Colin Kite (Smith), John Pearmain (Farrier).

—.—.—— **The Final Last**   R1 / 40
Alternative transmissions: BBC 2: 30.10.1967
Written by Peter Nelson; directed by Sybil Moore.
Adrian Oz (Mr Jenkins), Alan Hurley (Collier), Annalisé Moore (Juanita), Laurence Brazen (Mr Talmadge), Robert Plume (The Baron), Adrian Balance (Settle), Peter Scale*.

Each entry has a similar pattern. It starts with a transmission date, and possibly a transmission time – assuming the episode was transmitted – and is followed by the episode title. Where a programme doesn't use episode titles, there will sometimes be a short synopsis in its place and these will always be put in "speech marks" like this. Other times, particularly when we have a longer synopsis, it will appear underneath the line with the episode title. Finally, we list the current archive holding status of the episode and the original transmission format where we know it. A list of archive and transmission format codes and other formatting symbols may be found at the end of this book.

Where additional or alternative transmission information is available for other channels or regions, this will be included next. Lastly, the credits and cast for the particular episode are shown, excluding any regulars who have already been listed at programme or series level. If a performer appears in almost every episode of a long running series, he or she will sometimes be credited at programme level as though in every episode and the episodes they did not appear in will carry a note "So-and-so did not appear in this episode". Lastly, you may see some cast or credit information marked with an asterisk as in Peter Scale's credit in the final episode listed above. This shows that the role in question was uncredited and, while we believe the information to be correct, in many cases this is based upon unpublished information and so may not be separately verifiable.

ANY QUESTIONS (RADIO)

A BBC production for BBC Radio 4. Transmission details are for BBC Radio 4.

Holding / Source

31.03.1972 20:30 – 21:15   J / Live

Production by Michael Bowen.

With David Jacobs (Chairman), Baroness Stocks, Lord Robens, Kenneth Allsop, Dickie Henderson.

From Liss, Hampshire.

THE ARTHUR ASKEY VARIETY SHOW (RADIO)

A BBC production for BBC Radio 2. Transmission details are for BBC Radio 2.

A series of programmes to celebrate Arthur's 80 years, in which he is joined by top stars, newcomers and some old friends.

Programme credit(s):   Script by Tony Hare; production by Richard Willcox.

Programme performer(s):   Arthur Askey (Host).

Holding / Source

07.04.1981 22:00 – 23:00 **Programme 1**   AA / AA

With Roy Walker, Sweet Substitute, The Jay Jays, Dickie Henderson, Max Harris Orchestra.

BBC SWING SESSION (RADIO)

A BBC production for BBC Light Programme. Transmission details are for BBC Light Programme.

SERIES 3

Holding / Source

02.08.1955 22:20 – 23:05 **Swing Session**   NR / Live

With Paul Carpenter (Compere), Oscar Rabin and his Band, Jan Fraser, Mel Gaynor, Johnny Worth, The Reg Wale Sextet, Dickie Henderson.

BEFORE YOUR VERY EYES!

A BBC production. Transmission details are for BBC Television.

Programme performer(s):   Arthur Askey.

SERIES 2

Duration: 30 minutes.

Season credit(s):   Written by Sid Colin, Talbot Rothwell and David Climie; designed by Michael Yates; production by Bill Ward.

Season performer(s):   With Diana Decker.

Holding / Source

18.02.1953 21:10 – 21:40   NR / Live

Orchestra conducted by Eric Robinson.

With Freda Bamford, Brian Reece, Dickie Henderson [as Dick Henderson Jnr].

04.03.1953 20:15 – 20:45   NR / Live

Orchestra conducted by Eric Robinson.

With Dickie Henderson, Freddie Mills, Dave Willis, Annie Ross, Nicky Kidd.

18.03.1953 20:45 – 21:15   NR / Live

Orchestra conducted by Eric Robinson.

With Dickie Henderson. A guest artist was billed but not named.

01.04.1953 21:20 – 21:50   NR / Live

Orchestra conducted by Eric Robinson.

With Dickie Henderson. A guest artist was billed but not named.

BERNARD DELFONT'S SUNDAY SHOW

An ATV production. Transmission details are for ITV. Duration: 50 minutes.

SERIES 1

Transmission details are for the ABC midlands region.

Holding / Source

19.07.1959 20:30 – 21:30 **The Dickie Henderson Show**   J

Designed by Lewis Logan; production by Albert Locke.

With Dickie Henderson (Host), Ruby Murray, The Romanos Brothers, Arthur Blake, Steve Arlen, The Billy Petch Dancers, Harold Collins and his Orchestra.

06.09.1959 21:05 – 22:05 **The Dickie Henderson Show**   J

Designed by Lewis Logan; production by Alan Tarrant.

With Dickie Henderson (Host), Freddie Mills, The Piero Brothers, Neil and Pat Delrina, The Malcolm Mitchell Trio, Bertie Hare, The Deep River Boys, The Irving Davies Dancers, Harold Collins and his Orchestra.

SERIES 2

Transmission details are for the ABC midlands region.

Holding / Source

26.06.1960   J

Designed by Jon Scoffield; produced by Albert Locke.

With Dickie Henderson (Host), Jane Morgan, The Blackburn Twins, Jerry Collins, The Malcolm Mitchell Trio, Harold Collins and his Orchestra.

03.07.1960   J

Dance direction by Irving Davies; designed by Jon Scoffield; produced by Francis Essex.

With Dickie Henderson (Host), Eve Boswell, Gianni Jaia, Jimmy Wheeler, The Irving Davies Dancers, Harold Collins and his Orchestra.

07.08.1960   J

Designed by Richard Lake; produced by Albert Locke.

With Dickie Henderson (Host), Roy Castle, Vicky Autier, The Peters Sisters, Harold Collins and his Orchestra.

14.08.1960   J

Dance direction by Malcolm Goddard; designed by Richard Lake and Philip Hickie; produced by Francis Essex.

With Dickie Henderson (Host), Ruby Murray, The Clark Brothers, Robert Beatty, George Moon, Freddie Mills, The Botonds, The Malcolm Goddard Dancers, Harold Collins and his Orchestra.

04.09.1960   J

Choreography by George Carden; designed by Henry Graveney; produced by Albert Locke.

With Dickie Henderson (Host), Senor Wences, Adele Leigh, Steve Arlen, The George Carden Dancers, Harold Collins and his Orchestra.

BID FOR FAME

An ABC production. Transmission details are for the ABC midlands region.

A nationwide search for talent looking for new artists in every field of entertainment. Valuable prizes and help in their careers will go to the successful contestants.

SERIES 1

Duration: 26 minutes.

Holding / Source

25.11.1956 15:45 – 16:15   J / Live

Introduced by Dickie Henderson.

02.12.1956 15:45 – 16:15   J / Live

Introduced by Dickie Henderson.

09.12.1956 15:45 – 16:15   J / Live

Introduced by Dickie Henderson; produced by Alick Hayes and David Southwood; directed by Alick Hayes and David Southwood.

With Joe Loss and his Orchestra.

From the Palais de Dance, Bury.

16.12.1956 15:45 – 16:15   J / Live

Introduced by Dickie Henderson.

30.12.1956 15:45 – 16:15   J / Live

Introduced by Dickie Henderson; produced by Alick Hayes and David Southwood; directed by Alick Hayes and David Southwood.

With Joe Loss and his Orchestra.

From the Royal Hall, Harrogate.

06.01.1957 15:45 – 16:15   J / Live

Introduced by Dickie Henderson; produced by Alick Hayes and David Southwood; directed by Alick Hayes and David Southwood.

With Joe Loss and his Orchestra.

From ABC Television Studios, Manchester.

13.01.1957 15:45 – 16:15   J / Live

Introduced by Dickie Henderson; produced by Alick Hayes and David Southwood; directed by Alick Hayes and David Southwood.

With Joe Loss and his Orchestra, Rex Gray and Doreen Morgan, Jill and Jose Stewart, Long and Flower, Nina Yanson.

From the Hotel Leofric, Coventry.

20.01.1957 15:45 – 16:15   J / Live

Introduced by Dickie Henderson.

With Elaine Clifford, Bluenotes.

27.01.1957 15:45 – 16:15   J / Live

Introduced by Dickie Henderson; produced by Alick Hayes and David Southwood; directed by Alick Hayes and David Southwood.

With Joe Loss and his Orchestra.

From the Casino Ballroom, Leigh.

16.02.1957 18:20 – 19:00   J / Live

Introduced by Dickie Henderson; produced by Alick Hayes and David Southwood; directed by Alick Hayes and David Southwood.

With Joe Loss and his Orchestra, Dudley Freeman, The Smith Sisters, Patricia Sally, Sydney Warmsley, Barbara Helliwell.

BIG NIGHT OUT

An ABC production. Transmission details are for the ABC midlands region. Usual duration: 52 minutes.

SERIES 1

Duration: 40 minutes.

Holding / Source

29.07.1961   J

Choreography by Malcolm Goddard; designed by David Gillespie; directed by Bill Hitchcock.

With Dickie Henderson, Eve Boswell, Adele Leigh, The Clark Brothers, Freddie Mills, The Savoy Dancers, Bob Sharples and his Music, The Barney Gilbraith Singers.

THE BIG SHOW

A Black Brothers production for Tyne Tees Television. Transmission details are for the Tyne Tees region. Duration: 50 minutes.

Produced and directed by Bill Lyon-Shaw.

Dickie Henderson, Jill Day, Bill Maynard, Jack Payne, Bill Travers, Virginia McKenna, Linden Travers, Jimmy James, Dick Carlton, Eli Woods.

	Holding / Source
15.01.1959	DB-4W / 40

Shown on the opening night of the Tyne Tees television service. The existing recording of this programme includes part of the advert breaks both before, during and after the programme.

THE BIG SHOW

Alternative/Working Title(s): SHOWTIME '67 / SPOTLIGHT (Original title, on designers' schedules in 1967)

An ATV production. Transmission details are for the ATV London region. Duration: 50 minutes.

Transmission details are for the ABC midlands region.

	Holding / Source
05.05.1968	DB-NP / 2"

Written by Barry Cryer and Tony Hawes; music associates Derek Scott and Sam Harding; designed by Eric Shedden; produced by Jon Scoffield; directed by Philip Casson.

With Phyllis Diller, Michael Bentine, Alfred Ravel, Anita Harris, Dickie Henderson, The Five Luxors, The Shadows, Frankie Vaughan, The London Line, The Mike Sammes Singers, Jack Parnell and his Orchestra.

Production Date(s): **Recording**: 21.01.1968

If people ask ITV if they hold any editions of The Big Show they will say no. Ask them if they hold editions of Showtime '67, the USA title, and they say yes!

BIG-HEARTED ARTHUR (RADIO)

A BBC production for BBC Radio 2. Transmission details are for BBC Radio 2.

A tribute to the late Arthur Askey from his friends and fellow artists.

Introduced by Sir John Mills; research Gerald Frow; production by John Dyas.

Arthur Askey [Subject of Tribute], Leslie Crowther, Vernon Harris, Dickie Henderson, McDonald Hobley, Richard Murdoch, Cliff Richard, Jimmy Tarbuck, Tommy Trinder, Anthea Askey.

	Holding / Source
09.12.1982 19:30 – 20:30	AA / AA

THE BILLY COTTON BAND SHOW

A BBC production. Transmission details are for BBC Television.

Programme performer(s):   Billy Cotton (Host).

Duration: 45 minutes.

Season credit(s):   Written by Jimmy Grafton; orchestra conducted by Harry Rabinowitz; choreography by Leslie Roberts; associate producer Leslie Roberts; production by Johnnie Stewart.

	Holding / Source
20.10.1962	J

With Kathie Kay, Alan Breeze, The High-Lights, The Leslie Roberts Silhouettes, Dickie Henderson, John Leyton.

BILLY COTTON'S MUSIC HALL

A BBC production for BBC 1. Transmission details are for BBC 1. Duration: 45 minutes.

Programme credit(s):   Written by Eric Davidson.

Programme performer(s): Billy Cotton and his Band (Themselves), The Tiller Girls (Resident Dancers), The Cotton Singers (Resident Singers).

SERIES 1

Season credit(s):   Dances staged by Malcolm Goddard; designed by Colin Pigott; production by Michael Hurll.

Season performer(s): With Kathie Kay, Alan Breeze, The Cotton Singers, The Malcolm Goddard Dancers.

Holding / Source

23.10.1965   J / Live

Orchestra conducted by Harry Rabinowitz.

With Dickie Henderson, The Clancy Brothers with Tommy Makem, The Womenfolk, Mrs Mills, Rita Webb, Edmundson and Elliott.

SERIES 2

Season credit(s):   Orchestra conducted by Ronnie Hazlehurst; production by Michael Hurll.

Season performer(s): With Kathie Kay, The New Cotton Singers.

Holding / Source

10.07.1966   J / Live

Dances staged by Malcolm Goddard; designed by John Burrowes.

With Russ Conway, Frank Ifield, Dickie Henderson, Dave Allen.

BLACKPOOL NIGHT (RADIO)

A BBC production for BBC Light Programme. Transmission details are for BBC Light Programme.

SERIES 9

A BBC North production. Duration: 60 minutes.

Holding / Source

17.06.1959 20:30 – 21:30 **Programme 1**   J / AA

Orchestra conducted by Alyn Ainsworth; production by Roy Speer.

With Jack Watson (Host), Percy Edwards, Reginald Dixon, Jimmy Leach and Harry Hayward, Freddie Sales, Doreen Hume, Edmund Hockridge, Dickie Henderson, The Woodmen, BBC Northern Dance Orchestra.

THE BLACKPOOL SHOW

An ABC Manchester production for ABC. Transmission details are for the ABC midlands region. Duration: 52 minutes.

Spectacular from the summer home of show-business. From the stage of the ABC Theatre Blackpool.

SERIES 2

Season credit(s):   Written by Eric Merriman; choreography by Irving Davies.

Season performer(s): With Dickie Henderson (Compere), The Blackpool Show Dancers, Bob Sharples and his ABC Television Showband, Irving Davies.

Holding / Source

25.06.1967 22:05 – 23:05   J|a / 40

Designed by Terry Gough; produced and directed by Mark Stuart.

With Mel Tormé, Mike Newman, Patsy Ann Noble (Herself).

Extracts exist.

02.07.1967 22:05 – 23:05   J / 40

Additional material by Frank Roscoe; designed by Terry Gough; produced and directed* by Mark Stuart.

With Frank Ifield, The Beverly Sisters, Freddy Davies, Fred Roby, Louise Lenton.

09.07.1967 22:05 – 23:05   J / 40
Designed by Terry Gough; produced and directed* by Mark Stuart.
With Nancy Wilson, Bob Monkhouse, Johnny Hart, Kenny Ball and his Jazzmen, Louise Lenton.

16.07.1967 22:05 – 23:05   J / 40
Additional material by Frank Roscoe; designed by Harry Clark; produced and directed* by Mark Stuart.
With Dusty Springfield, Norm Crosby, Arthur Worsley, The Clark Brothers, Louise Lenton.

23.07.1967 22:05 – 23:05   J / 40
Designed by Terry Gough; produced and directed* by Mark Stuart.
With Frankie Howerd, Anita Harris, Hope and Keen, The Rockin' Berries, Louise Lenton.

30.07.1967 22:05 – 23:05   J / 40
Designed by Harry Clark; produced and directed* by Mark Stuart.
With The Shadows, Julie Rogers, Chris Kirby, Les Dawson.

06.08.1967 22:05 – 23:05   J / 40
Designed by Harry Clark; produced and directed* by Keith Beckett.
With Cilla Black, Jimmy Logan, Frank Sinatra Jr.

13.08.1967 22:05 – 23:05   JSEQ|a / 40
Designed by Harry Clark; produced and directed* by Keith Beckett.
With Frankie Vaughan, The New Faces, Les Dawson, Tanya [Elephant], Jenda Smaha, Basil Tait, The V Group.

2 extracts exists including the earliest surviving Les Dawson performance.

From the ABC Theatre, Blackpool.

BLANKETY BLANK

A BBC production for BBC 1, made in association with Mark Goodson / Talbot TV Ltd. Transmission details are for BBC 1.

Programme credit(s):   Theme music by Ronnie Hazlehurst.

SERIES 1

Duration: 35 minutes.

Season credit(s):   Programme associate Tony Hawes; designed by Bernard Lloyd-Jones; produced by Alan Boyd; directed by Marcus Plantin.

Season performer(s): With Terry Wogan (Host).

Holding / Source
03.05.1979 19:15 – 19:50   DB / 2"
With Lorraine Chase (Panellist), Val Doonican (Panellist), David Hamilton (Panellist), Dickie Henderson (Panellist), Karen Kay (Panellist), Elaine Stritch (Panellist).

THE BOB HOPE CLASSIC CABARET

An LWT production. Transmission details are for the ATV midlands region. Duration: 50 minutes.

Special variety show starring some of the celebrities who this week have been participating in the Bob Hope Golf Classic, from the Grosvenor Hotel, London. Staged by Dickie Henderson and Grosvenor Theatrical Productions in association with the Daily Express newspaper, in aid of the Stars' Organisation for Spastics - with Princess Margaret in attendance.

Produced by David Bell; directed by Alasdair MacMillan.

Bob Hope, Vic Damone, Iris Williams, Jimmy Tarbuck, David Soul, John Mills, Dickie Henderson, Foster Brooks.

Holding / Source
26.09.1981 21:15 – 22:15   D2 / 2"

BOB HOPE ROYAL GALA EVENING

A Grosvenor Theatrical Productions production for BBC 1. Transmission details are for BBC 1. Duration: 78 minutes.

Special variety show starring celebrities from the Grosvenor Hotel, London. Staged by Dickie Henderson and Grosvenor Theatrical Productions in aid of the Stars' Organisation for Spastics - with Princess Margaret in attendance.

Introduced by David Jacobs; additional material by Charlie Adams and Ken Ellis; musical director Ronnie Hazlehurst; executive producer Dickie Henderson; production manager Mike Pearce; produced by Yvonne Littlewood and Michael Gelardi; directed by Yvonne Littlewood.

Bob Hope, Charles Aznavour, Roy Budd, Dickie Henderson, Rich Little, The Nolan Sisters [as The Nolans], Eric Sykes, John Williams, Jonathan Winters, The Johnny Howard Orchestra, Bob Monkhouse, Tim Rice.

Holding / Source

12.10.1983   DB / 1"

Bob Monkhouse appears in the audience.

BOB MONKHOUSE

An ATV production. Untransmitted.

Bob Monkhouse, Michele Dotrice, Emu, Tony Adams, Don Maclean, Dickie Henderson.

Holding / Source

##.##.####   DB|n / 2"

Production Date(s): **Recording**: 14.09.1977

1977 production material for unmade series.

BRIAN RIX PRESENTS...

A BBC production for BBC 1. Transmission details are for BBC/BBC1. Usual duration: 90 minutes.

Transmission details are for BBC Television.

Holding / Source

05.06.1960 20:35 – 22:10 **Doctor in the House**   J

Duration: 95 minutes.

Adapted by Ted Willis; based on a book by Richard Gordon; produced by Mary Evans; directed by Wallace Douglas.

With Emrys James (John Evans), Dickie Henderson (Tony Grimsdyke), Helen Jessop (Vera), Brian Rix (Simon Sparrow), Charles Cameron (Sir Lancelot Spratt), Larry Noble (Bromley), Liz Fraser (Riggie), Fabia Drake (Matron), Sheila Hancock (Janet).

Recorded at the Whitehall Theatre

BRING ME SUNSHINE – A TRIBUTE TO ERIC MORECAMBE, OBE

A Thames Television production. Transmission details are for the Central region. Duration: 125 minutes.

Introduced by Ernie Wise from the London Palladium, in aid of the British Heart Foundation. In the presence of Prince Philip, Patron of the Foundation, and guest of honour Mrs Joan Morecambe, the stars pay tribute to a much-loved comedian who died earlier this year. The range and quality of artistes appearing make it an outstanding showbusiness event.

Introduced by Ernie Wise; written by Barry Cryer and Sid Colin; consultant Billy Marsh; designed by Peter Le Page; executive producers Philip Jones and Louis Benjamin; produced for the stage by Robert Nesbitt; directed by Mark Stuart.

Michael Aspel, Lionel Blair, Leslie Crowther, Dickie Davies, Bertice Reading, Wayne Sleep, Kenny Ball, Alison Bell, Max Bygraves, Cannon and Ball, James Casey, Roy Castle, Petula Clark, Barry Cryer, Suzanne Danielle, Jim Davidson, Frank Finlay, Bruce Forsyth, Jill Gascoine, Cherry Gillespie, Hannah Gordon, The Half Wits, Susan Hampshire, Dickie Henderson, Benny Hill, Diane Keen, Bonnie Langford, Lulu, Francis Matthews, Fulton Mackay, Nanette Newman, Des O'Connor, Mick Oliver, Elaine Paige, Michael Parkinson, Angela Rippon, Jimmy Tarbuck, John Thaw, The Tiller Girls, Arthur Tolcher, Bryn Williams, Eli Woods, Mike Yarwood, The Irving Davies Dancers, The Stephen Hill Singers.

	Holding / Source
25.12.1984 18:00 – 20:30	1" / 1"

CALLING MISS COURTNEIDGE (RADIO)

A BBC production for BBC Home Service. Transmission details are for BBC Home Service.

Laughter, drama and a song or two.

Programme credit(s):   Script by Gene Crowley; production by Alastair Scott-Johnston.

Programme performer(s): Cicely Courtneidge.

SERIES 1

Season credit(s):   Orchestra conducted by Harry Rabinowitz.

Season performer(s): With The Hedley Ward Trio, BBC Revue Orchestra.

	Holding / Source
09.12.1954 20:30 – 21:00 **Programme 8**	J / AA

With Robert Beatty, Vanessa Lee, Dickie Henderson, Jack Hulbert.

SERIES 2

Season credit(s):   Orchestra conducted by Paul Fenoulhet.

Season performer(s): With The Hedley Ward Trio, BBC Variety Orchestra.

	Holding / Source
27.04.1955 19:00 – 19:30 **Programme 7**	J / AA

With Maurice Denham and Gene Crowley, Dickie Henderson, John Cameron, Margaret Rawlings.

SERIES 3

Season performer(s): With The Hedley Ward Trio.

	Holding / Source
05.12.1955 19:00 – 19:30 **Programme 7**	J / AA

Orchestra conducted by Harry Rabinowitz.

With Joan Sims, Gene Crowley, Dickie Henderson, William Dickie, Nigel Patrick, BBC Revue Orchestra.

CELEBRITY SQUARES

Alternative/Working Title(s): BOB AND THE BIG BOX GAME! / BOB'S GALAXY GAME / BOB'S SUPERSQUARES / THE ATV SUNDAY QUIZ / THE BIG NAME GAME!

An ATV production. Transmission details are for the ATV midlands region. Duration: 39 minutes.

Programme credit(s):   Devised by Merrill Heatter and Bob Quigley; music by Jack Parnell.

Programme performer(s):   Bob Monkhouse (Presenter).

SERIES 1

Season credit(s):   Written by Dennis Berson; produced and directed by Paul Stewart Laing.

Season performer(s): With Kenny Everett (Voice Only).

Holding / Source

23.11.1975   J|a / 2"

Additional material by Peter Vincent; designed by Ray White.

With Spike Milligan (Contestant), William Rushton (Contestant), Sara Leighton (Contestant), Barbara Windsor (Contestant), Pat Coombs (Contestant), Robin Nedwell (Contestant), Paul Melba (Contestant), Michael Aspel (Contestant), Dickie Henderson (Contestant).

SERIES 2

Season credit(s):   Written by Dennis Berson; produced by Paul Stewart Laing.

Season performer(s): With Kenny Everett (Voice Only).

Holding / Source

26.03.1977 18:15 – 19:00   J / 2"

Designed by Bryan Holgate; directed by Paul Stewart Laing.

With Hinge & Bracket (Contestant), Pat Coombs (Contestant), Dickie Henderson (Contestant), Tom O'Connor (Contestant), Jean Rook (Contestant), Willy Rushton (Contestant), Keith Chegwin, Peter Goodwright, Elizabeth Harrison.

02.04.1977 18:15 – 19:00   J / 2"

Designed by Bryan Holgate; directed by Paul Stewart Laing.

With Dickie Henderson (Contestant), Colin Baker (Contestant), Diana Dors (Contestant), Arthur Mullard (Contestant), William Rushton (Contestant), Tessa Wyatt (Contestant), David Hamilton, Dukes & Lee, Alan Stewart.

28.05.1977 18:15 – 19:00   J|a / 2"

Additional material by Ian Messiter and Jeremy Beadle; designed by Bryan Holgate; directed by Paul Stewart Laing.

With Colin Baker (Contestant), Faith Brown (Contestant), Aimi MacDonald (Contestant), Diana Dors (Contestant), Dickie Henderson (Contestant), Arthur Mullard (Contestant), Doctor Magnus Pyke (Contestant), Willy Rushton (Contestant), Arthur Askey (Contestant).

04.06.1977 19:15 – 20:00   J|a / 2"

Additional material by Jeremy Beadle, Ian Messiter and Garry Chambers; designed by Bryan Holgate; directed by Christopher Tookey.

With Ray Alan and Lord Charles (Contestants), Katie Boyle (Contestant), Pat Coombs (Contestant), Les Dawson (Contestant), Michele Dotrice (Contestant), Dickie Henderson (Contestant), Willy Rushton (Contestant), Tony Adams, Christopher Beeny.

18.06.1977 19:15 – 20:00   J|a / 2"

Additional material by Jeremy Beadle, Ian Messiter and Garry Chambers; designed by Bryan Holgate; directed by Christopher Tookey.

With Faith Brown (Contestant), Joe Brown (Contestant), Dickie Davies (Contestant), Les Dawson (Contestant), Dickie Henderson (Contestant), Mollie Sugden (Contestant), Willy Rushton (Contestant), Jacquie-Ann Carr, Freddie Trueman.

THE CHRISTMAS HOUR

An Associated-Rediffusion production. Transmission details are for Associated-Rediffusion. Duration: 52 minutes.

Written by Jimmy Coghill, Bill Smith and Vic Hallums; special material by Abbe Gail and Martin Slavin; music by Steve Race and his Orchestra; orchestrations by Alan Braden and Martin Slavin; choreography by Malcolm Goddard; settings by Henry Federer; produced and directed by Eric Croall.

Hughie Green (Host), Winifred Atwell, David Blair, Allen Bruce, Fred Borders, Jean Clarke, Tommy Cooper, Plantagenent Somerset Fry, Ray Ellington, Lind Joyce, Dickie Henderson, Anthony Kerr, Rex North, Brian Reece, Ken Wilson, Ray Bennett, Joyce Blair, Harry Brunning, Jill Browne, Alma Cogan, Julie Demarco, Malcolm Goddard, McDonald Hobley, Marion Keene, Nadina Nerina, Veronica Page, Joan Rhodes, Georgie Wood, The Malcolm Goddard Dancers, Band of H.M. Irish Guards, The Barney Gilbraith Singers.

Holding / Source

25.12.1959 18:45 – 19:45   J

CILLA

A BBC production for BBC 1. Transmission details are for BBC 1. Usual duration: 50 minutes.

Programme performer(s):   Cilla Black (Host).

SERIES 1

Season credit(s):   Written by Ronnie Taylor; music by Ronnie Hazlehurst; produced by Michael Hurll.

Season performer(s): With The Irving Davies Dancers, The Ladybirds.

Holding / Source

20.02.1968   J / 2"

With Lulu, Ray Fell, Dickie Henderson.

SERIES 2

Season credit(s):   Choreography by Irving Davies; produced and directed by Michael Hurll.

Season performer(s): With The Irving Davies Dancers (Resident Dancers), The Breakaways (Resident Backing Singers).

Holding / Source

19.02.1969   R1

Designed by Roger Ford; outside broadcast director Vernon Lawrence.

With Cliff Richard, Dickie Henderson.

CINDERELLA

A Yorkshire Television production. Transmission details are for the ATV midlands region. Duration: 55 minutes.

Here's Cinderella with a difference. It's back to the good old days. Traditional pantomime without the modern idea of introducing pop groups and the like. Staged at the City Varieties Theatre, Leeds, it stars Dickie Henderson. And Dickie, like his father before him, has always been a traditionalist on the Christmas scene, with Buttons as his "speciality".

Adapted by Bert Gaunt and Jess Yates; based on a book by Derek Salberg; musical director Charles Smitton; designed by Ian McCrow; executive producer Jess Yates; produced and directed by Bill Hitchcock.

Susan George (Cinders), Vince Hill (Prince Charming), Lionel Blair (Dandini), Dickie Henderson (Buttons), John Inman (Ugly Sister), Barry Howard (Ugly Sister), Jack Douglas (Baron Stoneybroke), The Lionel Blair Dancers (Resident Dancers), The Mike Sammes Singers (Resident Backing Singers), Jean Pearce Sunbeams, The Tiddleywinks, Clive James.

Holding / Source

25.12.1970 16:40 – 17:35   J / 2"

COMEDY PARADE (RADIO)

A BBC production for BBC Radio various. Transmission details are for BBC Radio various. Duration: 30 minutes.

SERIES 2

A BBC production for BBC Light Programme. Transmission details are for BBC Light Programme.

Holding / Source

14.10.1965 20:00 – 20:30 **How About That?**   J / AA

Written by Bryan Blackburn; production by Edward Taylor.

With Dickie Henderson, Dilys Laye, Peter Reeves, Bryan Blackburn, Burt Rhodes and his Orchestra.

THE DAVE ALLEN SHOW

A BBC production for BBC 1. Transmission details are for BBC 1.

Programme cast: Dave Allen.

Duration: 45 minutes.

Season credit(s):   Musical director Norman Percival; choreography by Mavis Ascott.

Holding / Source

01.11.1969   J / 2"

Written by Eric Davidson, Bill Stark, Bernie Sharp and Dave Allen.

With Ed Nelson, Dickie Henderson, Maggie Fitzgibbon, Sylvia McNeill, Dick Garner, Mavis Ascott Dancers.

THE DAVID NIXON SHOW

A Thames Television production. Transmission details are for the ATV midlands region.

Programme performer(s): David Nixon (Host).

SERIES 4

Duration: 40 minutes.

Season credit(s):   Written by David Nixon and George Martin; musical director Ronnie Aldrich; magical adviser Ali Bongo; production associate George Martin; designed by Peter Elliott; produced and directed by Royston Mayoh.

Holding / Source

##.##.####   NR / NM

Originally scheduled for 26.05.1975.

With Dickie Henderson, Aimi MacDonald, Potassy and Assistant.

There was an edition scheduled for 26.05.75, but it was never produced due to a strike.

SERIES 5

Duration: 41 minutes.

Season credit(s):   Written by David Nixon and George Martin; musical director Ronnie Aldrich; music associate Don Hunt; magical adviser Ali Bongo; production associate George Martin; designed by Mike Hall; produced and directed by Royston Mayoh.

Holding / Source

19.04.1976   DB-D3 / 2"

With Trevor Lewis, Phoa Yan Tiong, Dickie Henderson.

DES O'CONNOR TONIGHT

A BBC production for BBC 2. Transmission details are for BBC 2. Usual duration: 50 minutes.

Programme performer(s):   Des O'Connor (Host).

SERIES 3

Season credit(s):   Programme associate Neil Shand; orchestra directed by Colin Keyes; designed by Anna Ridley; executive producer James Moir; produced and directed by Marcus Plantin.

Holding / Source

18.02.1980   DB-D3 / 2"

With Ronnie Schell, Iris Williams, Dickie Henderson.

THE DICKIE HENDERSON HALF-HOUR

A Jack Hylton TV Productions production for Associated-Rediffusion. Transmission details are for Associated-Rediffusion. Duration: 25 minutes.

Programme credit(s):   Produced and directed by Bill Hitchcock.

Programme performer(s):   Dickie Henderson (Dickie), Anthea Askey (Anthea), Eve Lister, Bernard Hunter.

SERIES 1

Season credit(s):   Written by Jack Greenhalgh; designed by Robert Freemantle.

Holding / Source

04.07.1958   R3N|n

Music by Steve Race and his Orchestra.

With Ilene Day, June Cunningham, Tom Payne, Claire Gordon, Eve Lister, Bernard Hunter.

Reel one exists on R3 for the edition.

11.07.1958   R3N|n

Music by Steve Race and his Orchestra.

With Freddie Mills, Eve Lister, Bernard Hunter, Ilene Day.

18.07.1958   R3N|n

Music by Steve Race and his Orchestra.

With Eric Delaney, Len Lowe, Diane Todd, Eve Lister, Bernard Hunter.

25.07.1958   R3N|n

Music by Steve Race and his Orchestra.

With Len Lowe, Jill Day, Eve Lister, Bernard Hunter.

01.08.1958   R3N|n

Music by Steve Race and his Orchestra.

With Patricia Moore, Eve Lister, Bernard Hunter, Len Lowe, Sara Leighton.

08.08.1958   R3N|n

Music by Steve Race and his Orchestra.

With William Sylvester, Sara Leighton, Eve Lister, Bernard Hunter, Len Lowe, Patsy Rowlands, Grace Webb, Marion Keene.

15.08.1958   R3NSEQ|n

Music by Steve Race and his Orchestra.

With Freddie Mills, Len Lowe, Ilene Day, Eve Lister, Bernard Hunter, John Abineri.

Reel two exists for the edition.

22.08.1958   R3N|n

Music by Steve Race and his Orchestra.

With Freddie Mills, Eve Lister, Bernard Hunter, Diane Todd.

29.08.1958	R3N|n

Music by Steve Race and his Orchestra.
With Marion Keene, Eve Lister, Bernard Hunter.

05.09.1958	R3N|n

Music by Billy Ternent and his Orchestra.
With Marion Keene, Eve Lister, Bernard Hunter.

12.09.1958	R3N|n

Music by Billy Ternent and his Orchestra.
With June Cunningham, Diane Todd, Bernard Hunter, Eve Lister.

SERIES 2

Season credit(s):   Script by Jack Hylton TV Scripts; script associate Jimmy Grafton; music by Billy Ternent and his Orchestra; designed by Denis Wreford.

Holding / Source

04.05.1959	R3N|n

With Clive Dunn, Eve Lister, Bernard Hunter, Marion Keene.

11.05.1959	R3N|n

With Clive Dunn, Eve Lister, Bernard Hunter, Marion Keene.

18.05.1959	R3N|n

With Clive Dunn, Eve Lister, Bernard Hunter, Renate Holm.

25.05.1959	R3N|n

With Lionel Murton, Eve Lister, Bernard Hunter.

01.06.1959	R3N|n

With Clive Dunn, Eve Lister, Bernard Hunter, Renate Holm.
Reel one exists on picture only and reel two is complete.

08.06.1959	R3N|n

With Marion Keene, Clive Dunn, Eve Lister, Bernard Hunter.
Reel one is complete, but reel two is picture only.

15.06.1959	R3N|n

With Marion Keene, Clive Dunn, Eve Lister, Bernard Hunter, Ronnie Corbett.

22.06.1959	R3N|n

With Freddie Mills, Lionel Murton, Eve Lister, Bernard Hunter.

25.12.1959 12:30 – 12:55
Script by Jack Hylton TV Scripts; script assistant Jimmy Grafton; designed by Denis Wreford; directed by Bill Hitchcock.
With Eve Lister, Bernard Hunter.

THE DICKIE HENDERSON SHOW

A Harry Foster TV Productions production for Associated-Rediffusion. Transmission details are for the ATV midlands region. Usual duration: 25 minutes.

Programme cast: Dickie Henderson (Dickie).

Holding / Source

##.##.#### **[untransmitted pilot]**	J / 40

Written by Jimmy Grafton; additional material by Jeremy Lloyd and Alan Fell; directed by Bill Hitchcock.
With June Laverick (June), Richard Wattis (Scoutmaster), Hughie Green (Quizmaster), Jeremy Hawk.
Lionel Murton does not appear in this episode.

SERIES 1

Season credit(s):   Musical director Steve Race; directed by Bill Hitchcock.
Season cast: With June Laverick (June), John Parsons (Richard), Lionel Murton (Jack).

Holding / Source

14.11.1960   **The Psychiatrist**   D3|n / R3
Written by Jimmy Grafton and Jeremy Lloyd; settings by Roy Walker.
With Alfred Marks, Pat Coombs, Judy Cornwell, Lindsay Scott Patton.

21.11.1960   **The Quiz**   J
Written by Jimmy Grafton, Jeremy Lloyd and Alan Fell; settings by Roy Walker.
With Hughie Green, Richard Wattis, Gwen Lewis, John Crocker, Gordon Phillott.

28.11.1960   **The Song**   J
Written by Jimmy Grafton and Jeremy Lloyd; settings by Roy Walker.
With Marty Wilde, Meier Tzelniker, Pamela Greer, Elfrida Eden, Rex Grey, Benice Swanson, Albert Barnett.

05.12.1960   **The Dress**   J
Written by Jimmy Grafton and Jeremy Lloyd; story by Pip Baker and Jane Baker; settings by Roy Walker.
With Eve Boswell, Geoffrey Hibbert, John Crocker, Lindsay Scott Patton, Lisa Noble, Fiona Glenn.
Lionel Murton does not appear in this episode.

12.12.1960   **The Bachelor**   J
Executive writer Jimmy Grafton; associate writer Jeremy Lloyd; settings by Roy Walker.
With Michael Medwin, Sheena Marshe, Zena Marshall, David Ludman.

19.12.1960   **The Race**   J
Executive writer Jimmy Grafton; associate writers Jeremy Lloyd and Alan Fell; settings by Roy Walker.
With Richard Wattis, Robert Perceval, John Crocker, Hamlyn Benson, Ian Wilson, Beckett Bould, Stanley

26.12.1960 20:00 – 20:30 **The Diet**   J
Written by Jimmy Grafton; additional material by Jeremy Lloyd; orchestrations by Alan Braden; choreography
by Jane Dore; settings by Roy Walker.
With Jill Day, Douglas Robinson, Sheena Marshe, Valentino Musetti, Jane Dore, Judy Collins, Mariella Capes,
Clare Collins.

02.01.1961   **The Film Star**   J
Executive writer Jimmy Grafton; associate writer Jeremy Lloyd; orchestrations by Alan Braden; settings by
Roy Walker.
With Peter Graves, Sheila Hancock, David Ludman, Charles Irwin, Michael Adrian, Susan Denny.

09.01.1961   **The Fur Coat**   J
Executive writer Jimmy Grafton; associate writers Teddy Prior and Jeremy Lloyd; settings by Roy Walker.
With Pearl Carr, Teddy Johnson, Diana Beaumont, Ronnie Corbett, Arthur Mullard, Gwen Lewis, Garard
Green, Ralph Tovey, Tony Verner.
No Lionel Murton.

16.01.1961   **The Music Lovers**   J
Executive writer Jimmy Grafton; associate writers Jeremy Lloyd and Robert Gray; orchestrations by Alan
Braden; settings by Roy Walker.
With Adele Leigh, Edward Malin, Pat Coombs.

23.01.1961   **The Actor**   J
Executive writer Jimmy Grafton; associate writers Jeremy Lloyd and Stan Mars; orchestrations by Alan
Braden; settings by Roy Walker.
With Bernard Bresslaw, Frank Leighton, John McLaren, Lorne Cossette.

30.01.1961   **The Idol**   J
Executive writer Jimmy Grafton; associate writer Jeremy Lloyd; orchestrations by Alan Braden; settings by Roy Walker.
With John Bentley, Lindsay Scott Patton, Norma Parnell, Joel Noble.

06.02.1961   **The Farce**   J
Executive writer Jimmy Grafton; associate writers Jeremy Lloyd and Stan Mars; settings by Roy Walker.
With Elspet Gray, Brian Rix, Lindsay Scott Patton, Geoffrey Hibbert, David Ludman, Harry Littlewood, Pat Laurence, Pat Roberts, Irene Barrie.

13.02.1961   **The Golf Match**   J
Executive writer Jimmy Grafton; associate writer Jeremy Lloyd; orchestrations by Alan Braden; settings by Sylva Nadolny.
With Ted Ray, Harry Weetman, Gordon Rollings.

20.02.1961   **The Fight**   J
Executive writer Jimmy Grafton; associate writers Jeremy Lloyd and Robert Gray; orchestrations by Alan Braden; settings by Sylva Nadolny.
With Freddie Mills, Leo Britt, Blanche Moore, Gabrielle Daye, Sandra Le Brocq, Christine Childs.

27.02.1961   **The Violin**   J
Executive writer Jimmy Grafton; associate writers Jeremy Lloyd and Eric Newman; orchestrations by Alan Braden; settings by Sylva Nadolny.
With Vic Oliver, Alexander Doré, John Crocker.

06.03.1961   **The Move**   J
Executive writer Jimmy Grafton; associate writers Jeremy Lloyd and Eric Newman; orchestrations by Alan Braden; settings by Sylva Nadolny.
With Gladys Henson, Peter Barkworth, Gordon Phillott, Gordon Rollings, Nan Braunton, Gabrielle Daye, Marie Makino, Anthea Wyndam, David Ludman, Ernest Bale.

13.03.1961   **The Dancer**   J
Executive writer Jimmy Grafton; associate writers Jeremy Lloyd and Eric Newman; settings by Sylva Nadolny.
With Lionel Blair, Diana French, Kenneth Nash.

20.03.1961   **The Birthday Present**   J
Executive writer Jimmy Grafton; associate writers Jeremy Lloyd, Alan Fell and Stanley Myers; orchestrations by Alan Braden; settings by Sylva Nadolny.
With Richard Caldicot, Naunton Wayne, George Tovey, John Rae, Eric Nicholson, Arthur Blake.

27.03.1961   **The Relation**   J
Executive writer Jimmy Grafton; associate writers Jeremy Lloyd, Alan Fell and Stanley Myers; orchestrations by Alan Braden; settings by Sylva Nadolny.
With Pat Coombs, Irene Handl, Stuart Sanders, John Crocker, Michael Anthony, Beckett Bould.

03.04.1961   **The Burglars**   J
Executive writer Jimmy Grafton; associate writer Stan Mars; orchestrations by Alan Braden; settings by Sylva Nadolny.
With Donald Gray, Ivor Salter, Eugenie Cavanagh, James McLoughlin, Henry Kay.

10.04.1961   **The Maid**   R1
Executive writer Jimmy Grafton; associate writer Robert Gray; orchestrations by Alan Braden; settings by Sylva Nadolny.
With Neville Barker, Carole Shelley, Geoffrey Hibbert, Gwen Lewis.
Held by TDA/Kaleidosscope.

17.04.1961   **The Patient**   J
Executive writer Jimmy Grafton; associate writers Jeremy Lloyd and Stan Mars; orchestrations by Alan Braden; designed by Sylva Nadolny.
With Alan Melville, Joyce Barbour, Barbara Robinson, John Crocker, Gordon Rollings, Vikki Harrington.

24.04.1961 **The Rival** J

Executive writer Jimmy Grafton; associate writers Jeremy Lloyd and Stanley Myers; orchestrations by Alan Braden; choreography by Lionel Blair; settings by Sylva Nadolny.

With Conrad Phillips, Ronnie Corbett, George Tovey, Vi Stevens, Eugenie Cavanagh.

01.05.1961 **The Butler** J

Executive writer Jimmy Grafton; associate writers Jeremy Lloyd and Stan Mars; orchestrations by Alan Braden; settings by Sylva Nadolny.

With Arthur Askey, Robert Perceval, Donald Stewart, Lindsay Scott Patton, Jeremy Lloyd.

08.05.1961 **The Exchange Visit** J

Executive writer Jimmy Grafton; associate writers Jeremy Lloyd and Robert Gray; orchestrations by Alan Braden; designed by Sylva Nadolny.

With George Baker, Marie France, Edwina Mitchell, Rowena Torrence, Blanche Moore, Margaret Boyd, Benn Simons, Nicholas Roylance.

SERIES 2

Season credit(s): Written by Jimmy Grafton; musical director Steve Race; directed by Bill Hitchcock.

Season cast: With June Laverick (June), John Parsons (Richard), Lionel Murton (Jack).

Holding / Source

13.11.1961 **The Publicity Agent** J

Alt.Title(s): *Publicity*

Additional material by Jeremy Lloyd and Stanley Myers.

With Alfred Marks, Geoffrey Hibbert, Yvonne Ball.

20.11.1961 **The Record** J

Additional material by Robert Gray and Jeremy Lloyd; designed by David Catley.

With David Jacobs, Alexander Doré, Billy Milton.

27.11.1961 **The Plane** J

Additional material by Jeremy Lloyd and Stan Mars; designed by David Catley.

With Hughie Green.

04.12.1961 **The Camp** J

Additional material by Jeremy Lloyd; designed by David Catley.

With Richard Wattis, Betty Huntley-Wright, Robert Perceval, John Wentworth, Irene Richmond, Lindsay Scott Patton, Robin Ford.

11.12.1961 **The Paris Weekend** J

Additional material by Jeremy Lloyd.

With Sheena Marshe, Rudolph Offenbach, Howard Greene.

18.12.1961 **The Racehorse** J

Additional material by Alan Fell and Stanley Myers; designed by David Catley.

With Bill Owen, John Rickman, Joe Ritchie, Charles Farrell, Hamlyn Benson, William Douglas.

26.12.1961 20:00 – 20:30 **The Puppy** J

Additional material by Jeremy Lloyd; orchestrations by Alan Braden; edited by Ray Helm; designed by David Catley.

With no guest cast.

##.##.#### **The Fortune Teller** J

Additional material by Eric Newman and Stanley Myers.

With Ethel Revnell, Clifford Stanton.

Production Date(s): **Recording**: 22.12.1961

SERIES 3

Season credit(s):	Executive writer Jimmy Grafton; musical director Steve Race; orchestrations by Alan Braden; settings by David Catley.
Season cast:	With June Laverick (June), John Parsons (Richard), Lionel Murton (Jack).

Holding / Source

07.05.1962   **The Tramp**   J
Associate writer Eric Newman; directed by Bill Hitchcock.
With Frank Pettingell, Geoffrey Hibbert, Rita Webb, Victor Charrington, Howard Knight.

14.05.1962   **The New TV**   J
Associate writers Jeremy Lloyd and Robert Gray; directed by Ronald Marriott.
With Roy Castle, Mimi Law, Billy Whittaker.
Recorded 08.12.61 as part of the block of episodes that formed series 2.

21.05.1962   **The Necklace**   J
Associate writer Eric Newman; directed by Bill Hitchcock.
With Dora Bryan, Peter Welch, Gordon Rollings, Ronnie Corbett.

28.05.1962   **The Cure**   J
Postponed from 01.01.1962. Alternative transmissions: 01.01.1962: Associated-Rediffusion.
Associate writers Jeremy Lloyd and Stan Mars; directed by Bill Hitchcock.
With Eve Boswell.
Recorded 17.11.61 as part of the block of episodes that formed series 2.

04.06.1962   **The Protest**   J
Associate writers Stanley Myers and Alan Fell; directed by Bill Hitchcock.
With Brian Oulton, James Hayter, Mollie Maureen, Pat Coombs, Joe Ritchie, Frank Sieman.

11.06.1962   **The Gangster**   J
Associate writers Jeremy Lloyd and Stan Mars; directed by Bill Hitchcock.
With Boris Karloff, John Crocker, Howard Knight, Danny Green, Fred McNaughton, John Barrard.

18.06.1962   **The Voyage**   J
Associate writers Jeremy Lloyd and Stan Mars; directed by Bill Hitchcock.
With George Coulouris, Tom Gill, Frank Sieman, Ronnie Corbett, Robert Cawdron, Dorothea Phillips, Walter Swash.

SERIES 4

Season credit(s):	Executive writer Jimmy Grafton; musical director Steve Race; orchestrations by Alan Braden; settings by David Catley; directed by Bill Hitchcock.
Season cast:	With June Laverick (June), John Parsons (Richard), Lionel Murton (Jack).

Holding / Source

21.11.1962   **The Footballer**   J
Associate writers Eric Newman and Stan Mars.
With Danny Blanchflower, George Tovey, Douglas Blackwell, Paul Carpenter.

28.11.1962   **The Visit**   J
Associate writers Stanley Myers and Alan Fell.
With Beryl Reid, Tom Gill, Peter Elliott, William Dysart, Stanley Ayres.
Lionel Murton does not appear in this episode.

05.12.1962   **The Beauty Contest**   J
Associate writers Stanley Myers and Alan Fell.
With Peter Barkworth, Carole Shelley, Valerie Brooks, Raymond Adamson, Harry Littlewood.

12.12.1962   **The Romance**   D3-R1|n
With Richard Wattis.

19.12.1962   **The Leprechaun**   J
Associate writers Eric Newman and Stan Mars.
With Ruby Murray, Bobby Howes, Y Diliau, Bee Duffell, John Kelly, Michael Corcoran, Francis Napier.

25.12.1962 20:00 – 21:00 **The Dickie Henderson Christmas Show**   J
Duration: 50 minutes.
Written by Jimmy Grafton and Jeremy Lloyd; dance direction by Pamela Devis.
With John Parsons (Richard), Lionel Murton (Jack), Bernard Bresslaw, Hughie Green, Alfred Marks, Richard Wattis, Leslie Sarony, Joe Ritchie, William Douglas, Harry Littlewood, Helen Ford, Lindsay Scott Patton, Susan George, David Palmer, The Ivor Raymonde Singers, The Pamela Devis Dancers.
Recorded in two parts, on 27.10.62 and 19.10.62.

02.01.1963   **The Addict**   J
Associate writer Stanley Myers.
With Ted Ray, Harry Westman, Gordon Rollings.

09.01.1963   **The Court Case**   J
Associate writers Stanley Myers and Alan Fell.
With Stanley Unwin, Michael Denison, Jeremy Lloyd, John Rae, John Crocker, Bob Todd, Alexandra Dane.

16.01.1963   **The Stamp Collector**   1"-R1|n
Associate writer Eric Newman.
With George Benson, Deryck Guyler, Fred Stone.

23.01.1963   **The Moonshiners**   J
Associate writers Jeremy Lloyd and Stan Mars.
With Jimmy Logan, John Rae, Jameson Clark.

30.01.1963   **The Quarrel**   J
Associate writer Eric Newman.
With Sheila Hancock.
 Held by Kaleidoscope.

06.02.1963   **The Double**   J
Associate writers Stanley Myers and Alan Fell.
With Bob Monkhouse, Golda Casimir, Viviane Ventura, Norman Chappell.

13.02.1963   **The Legacy**   J
Associate writers Stanley Myers and Alan Fell.
With John Parsons (Richard), Lionel Murton (Jack), Billy Danvers, John Crocker, John Cross, Paul Williamson, Arthur Blake, Naunton Wayne.

20.02.1963   **The Racing Car**   J
Associate writer Eric Newman.
With Lionel Murton (Jack), John Parsons (Richard), John Bolster, Anthony Bygraves, Jack Brabham.

13.03.1963   **The Hypnotist**   J
Associate writers Stan Mars and Peter Griffiths.
With John Parsons (Richard), Lionel Murton (Jack), Jon Pertwee, Tom Gill, Liza Page, Gwen Lewis, Eric Nicholson, Gordon Phillott, Margaret Boyd, Brenda Haydn.

27.03.1963   **The Housekeeper**   J
Associate writer Eric Newman.
With John Parsons (Richard), Lionel Murton (Jack), Jerry Desmonde, Irene Handl, Paul Williamson, Blanche Moore.

10.04.1963   **The Playwright**   J
Associate writers Johnny Whyte and Eric Newman.
With Lionel Murton (Jack), Michael Logan, Robert Cawdron, Dora Bryan.

| 17.04.1963 | **The Letter** | J |

Associate writer Jeremy Lloyd.

With Margaret Lockwood, John Rae, Pat Coombs.

| 24.04.1963 | **The Stately Home** | DB-R3|n |

Associate writers Stan Mars and Jeremy Lloyd.

With Lionel Murton (Jack), John Parsons (Richard), The Marquess of Bath, Andrew Bowen, Paul Williamson, Tom Gill.

SERIES 5

Season credit(s):   Musical director Steve Race; settings by David Catley; directed by Bill Hitchcock.

Season cast: With June Laverick (June), Lionel Murton (Jack).

Holding / Source

| 14.06.1963 | **The Crook** | J |

Executive writer Jimmy Grafton; associate writers Stanley Myers and Alan Fell; orchestrations by Alan Braden; edited by Roy Haydon.

With Raymond Francis (Detective Chief Superintendent Tom Lockhart), Paul Williamson, Arthur Gomez, Victor Charrington.

Recorded 01.03.1963 as part of the same production block as the episodes in broadcast series four.

| 21.06.1963 | **The Guinea Pigs** | J |

Executive writer Jimmy Grafton; associate writers Jeremy Lloyd and Stan Mars.

With John Parsons (Richard), Hamilton Dyce, Arthur Mullard, Jeremy Lloyd, Gwen Lewis, Paul Williamson, Alan Melville.

Recorded 15.03.1963 as part of the same production block as the episodes in broadcast series four.

| 28.06.1963 | **The Country Cottage** | J |

Executive writer Jimmy Grafton; associate writers Stanley Myers and Alan Fell; orchestrations by Alan Braden; edited by Ray Helm.

With John Parsons (Richard), Reginald Beckwith, Frank Sieman, James Hayter.

Recorded 22.03.1963 as part of the same production block as the episodes in broadcast series four.

| 05.07.1963 | **The Spy** | J |

Executive writer Jimmy Grafton; associate writers Jeremy Lloyd and Stan Mars; orchestrations by Alan Braden; edited by Ray Helm.

With John Parsons (Richard), Malcolm Webster, Rudolf Offenbach, Guy Doleman.

Recorded 04.04.1963 as part of the same production block as the episodes in broadcast series four.

| ##.##.#### | **The Painter** | J |

Originally scheduled for 12.07.1963. Alternative transmissions: 08.08.1963 18:15 – 18:45: Associated-Rediffusion.

Executive writer Jimmy Grafton; associate writers Stanley Myers and Alan Fell; orchestrations by Alan Braden; edited by Roy Haydon.

With John Parsons (Richard), Peter Elliott, Imogen Hassall, Lance Percival.

Replaced by an episode of Boyd Q.C. on 12.07.1963 on Associated-Rediffusion and, presumably, most other regions too given that this episode made the Network Top 20.

| 19.07.1963 | **The Convict** | J |

Executive writer Jimmy Grafton; associate writers Jeremy Lloyd and Stan Mars.

With George Tovey, Raymond Hodge, Gabrielle Daye, George Coulouris.

| 26.07.1963 | **The Wrestler** | J |

Executive writer Jimmy Grafton; associate writer Eric Newman; orchestrations by Alan Braden; edited by Ray Helm.

With John Parsons (Richard), Jackie Pallo, John Yearsley, Peter Szakacs, David Brown, Freddie Mills.

02.08.1963   **The School Play**   J
Executive writer Jimmy Grafton; associate writers Stanley Myers and Alan Fell.
With John Parsons (Richard), Damaris Hayman, Howard Knight, Richard Wattis.

19.09.1963   **The Parking Meter**   R3N|n
Executive writer Jimmy Grafton; associate writers Jeremy Lloyd, Stanley Myers and Alan Fell.
With Danny Grover (Richard).

26.09.1963   **The Babysitter**   J
Executive writer Jimmy Grafton; associate writers Jeremy Lloyd, Stanley Myers and Alan Fell.

03.10.1963   **The Home Doctor**   J
Executive writer Jimmy Grafton; associate writer Jeremy Lloyd.
With Paul Williamson, June Elvin.

10.10.1963   **The Husband Test**   J
Executive writer Jimmy Grafton; associate writer Jeremy Lloyd.
With Robert Sansom, Peter Elliot, Jane Murdoch, Norman Mitchell.

17.10.1963   **The Learner Driver**   R1|n
Written by Jimmy Grafton and Jeremy Lloyd.
With Richard Caldicot, John Rae, Malcolm Webster.

24.10.1963   **The Economy Campaign**   J
Written by Jimmy Grafton and Jeremy Lloyd.
With Danny Grover (Richard).

31.10.1963   **The Smugglers**   J
Written by Jimmy Grafton and Jeremy Lloyd.
With Danny Grover (Richard), Eddie Byrne.

07.11.1963   **The Old Flame**   J
Written by Jimmy Grafton and Jeremy Lloyd.
With Peter Graves, Eleanor Summerfield, Brenda Haydn, Don McCorkindale.
Lionel Murton does not appear in this episode.

14.11.1963   **The Fourteen Year Itch**   J
Written by Jimmy Grafton and Jeremy Lloyd.
With Eleanor Summerfield, Valerie Brooks.

21.11.1963   **The Treatment**   J
Written by Jimmy Grafton and Jeremy Lloyd.
With Ronnie Stevens, Jane Murdoch, Jennifer Woods, Damaris Hayman.

28.11.1963   **The Telephone**   J
Written by Jimmy Grafton, Stanley Myers and Alan Fell.
With Danny Grover (Richard), Joyce Barbour, Gordon Rollings.

05.12.1963   **The Gambler**   J
Written by Jimmy Grafton and Jeremy Lloyd.
With Danny Grover (Richard), Norman Chappell.

12.12.1963   **The White Lie**   J
Written by Jimmy Grafton and Jeremy Lloyd.
With Danny Grover (Richard), Guy Kingsley Poynter, Richard McNeff, Robert Perceval.

19.12.1963   **The Germ**   J
Written by Jimmy Grafton and Jeremy Lloyd.
With Danny Grover (Richard), Robert Raglan, Arthur Gomez.

26.12.1963 19:30 – 20:00 **The Sleepless Night**   J

When Dickie is so excited about a turn offer that he suffers from insomnia, his efforts to get to sleep produce some extraordinary results.

Written by Jimmy Grafton and Jeremy Lloyd.

With Danny Grover (Richard), Sheena Marshe, Rudolf Offenbach, John Bloomfield, Michael Segal.

SERIES 6

Season credit(s):   Musical director Steve Race; designed by David Catley; directed by Bill Hitchcock.

Season cast: With June Laverick (June), Lionel Murton (Jack).

		Holding / Source

29.04.1964   **The Green Eye**   DV

Written by Jimmy Grafton and Jeremy Lloyd.

With Danny Grover (Richard), Lionel Murton, William Franklyn, Anne Jameson, Geraldine Ward.

20.05.1964   **The Job**   J

Written by Jimmy Grafton and Jeremy Lloyd.

With Frank Thornton, Sheena Marshe, Rita Webb.

27.05.1964   **The Gift**   J

Written by Jimmy Grafton and Jeremy Lloyd.

With Danny Grover (Richard), Rita Webb, Jeremy Lloyd, Damaris Hayman, Anne Jameson, Norman Mitchell, The Frank and Peggy Spencer Formation Team.

03.06.1964   **Who Needs Who**   DB-R1|n

Written by Jimmy Grafton, Jeremy Lloyd and Maurice Wiltshire.

With Danny Grover (Richard), Eleanor Summerfield (Madge), Arthur Mullard, Barney Gilbraith.

10.06.1964   **When the Cat's Away**   J

Written by Jimmy Grafton and Jeremy Lloyd.

With Eleanor Summerfield (Madge), Robert Perceval (George), Hugh Latimer.

17.06.1964   **The Surprise**   DB-R1|n

Written by Jimmy Grafton and Jeremy Lloyd.

With Eleanor Summerfield (Madge), David Langton, Lizbeth Webb.

22.06.1964   **The Fan**   J

Written by Jimmy Grafton and Jeremy Lloyd.

With Norman Chappell, Hazel Coppen, Jane Murdoch.

08.07.1964   **Little Things Mean a Lot**   J

Written by Jimmy Grafton and Jeremy Lloyd.

With Eleanor Summerfield (Madge), Robert Perceval (George), Vic Oliver, Hugh Latimer.

05.08.1964   **The Moustache**   J

Postponed from 01.06.1964.

Written by Jimmy Grafton and Jeremy Lloyd.

With Danny Grover (Richard), Eleanor Summerfield (Madge), David Langton, Rudolf Offenbach, Shirley Cameron, Susanna Carroll, Cameron Hall, Rosemarie Frankland.

12.08.1964   **The Memory**   DB-R1|n

Postponed from 15.07.1964.

Written by Jimmy Grafton and Jeremy Lloyd.

With Eleanor Summerfield (Madge), Robert Perceval (George), Arthur Gomez.

SERIES 7

	Holding / Source
Season credit(s): Written by Jimmy Grafton and Jeremy Lloyd; designed by David Catley; directed by Bill Hitchcock.	
Season cast: With June Laverick (June), Lionel Murton (Jack).	

		Holding / Source
29.04.1965		J

With no guest cast.

		Holding / Source
06.05.1965		J

With no guest cast.

		Holding / Source
##.##.####		J

Alternative transmissions: 13.05.1965: Rediffusion Television.
With no guest cast.

		Holding / Source
20.05.1965	**Son of Dickie**	J

With Robert Scott Webber, June Elvin, Arthur Blake.

		Holding / Source
##.##.####	**The Dreamer**	J

Written by David Climie; script editor Jeremy Lloyd.
With Eleanor Summerfield (Madge), Frank Sieman.
Production Date(s): **Recording**: 24.01.1964

		Holding / Source
##.##.####	**The Father Figure**	J

Written by Jimmy Grafton and Jeremy Lloyd.
With Eleanor Summerfield (Madge), Danny Grover, Robert Perceval.
Production Date(s): **Recording**: 20.03.1964

		Holding / Source
##.##.####	**The Invitation**	J

Written by Jimmy Grafton and Jeremy Lloyd.
With Eleanor Summerfield (Madge), Gwen Lewis, Geoffrey Wincott.
Production Date(s): **Recording**: 23.10.1964

This brief series was scheduled as a replacement for Double Your Money which was postponed at short notice following a car accident which hospitalised Hughie Green. This change was too late for the listings magazines for the first two or three weeks and the national newspapers are divided on whether the episode shown in other regions on 13.05.65 was also shown in the midlands. Double Your Money would return, but only for a short run, on 27.05.65. The three episodes listed at the end of this block were all recorded in 1964 but we have been unable to find transmission dates; the temptation is to assume that they formed the first three in this series, albeit not necessarily in the order shown, as we can find no other likely candidates.

		Holding / Source
##.##.####	**[untransmitted pilot]**	J

Written by Jimmy Grafton and Jeremy Lloyd; directed by Bill Hitchcock.
With Lionel Murton, Peggy Cummins, Eileen Gourlay, Yolande Turner, Davy Kaye, Chic Murray, Peter Graves.
Recorded 15.04.1965. June Laverick does not appear in this episode.

SERIES 8

Season credit(s):	Written by Jimmy Grafton and Jeremy Lloyd; musical director Steve Race; settings by David Catley; directed by Bill Hitchcock.
Season cast:	With June Laverick (June), Lionel Murton (Jack Meadows).

		Holding / Source
16.08.1965	**The Marriage Contract**	R1

With Eleanor Summerfield, Hugh Latimer, Robert Perceval, Lizbeth Webb.

		Holding / Source
23.08.1965	**The Fortune Hunters**	J

With Danny Grover, Hugh Latimer, Peter Graves, Bertie Hare, Arthur Gross, Mark Gascoign, Kevin Bennett, Peter Pike, Janette Sattler.

30.08.1965	**The Cricketers**	J

With Freddie Trueman, Danny Grover, Bertie Hare.

06.09.1965	**The Shoppers**	J

With Eleanor Summerfield, Robert Perceval, Tom Gill, Felicity Gordon, Arthur Mullard, Blanche Moore, Claire Ruane.

13.09.1965	**The Love Letters**	R1

With Norma Foster.

Held in a private collection.

20.09.1965	**The Dogsbody**	J

With Semprini, Joseph Layode.

27.09.1965	**The Coward**	J

With Hugh Latimer, Lizbeth Webb, George Coulouris, Guy Kingsley Poynter, Jane Murdoch, Frank Sieman.

04.10.1965	**The Tangled Web**	J

With Eleanor Summerfield, Robert Perceval, Robert Raglan.

SERIES 9

Transmission details are for the ABC midlands region.

Season credit(s): Musical director Derek Warne; directed by Bill Hitchcock.

Season cast: With Isla Blair (Jane Henderson).

Holding / Source

26.11.1967 19:25 – 19:55 **What Happened Behind the Gym** J
Alt.Title(s): *It All Happened Behind The Gym*
Written by Jimmy Grafton and Jeremy Lloyd; designed by Bernard Goodwin.

With Peter Haigh (Himself), June Whitfield (Pauline Hurst), David Kelsey (Paul Hurst), Janet Brown (Zsa Zsa Gabbler), Trevor Lawrence (Rick Dagger).

03.12.1967 19:25 – 19:55 **The Image** J
Written by Jimmy Grafton and Jeremy Lloyd; designed by Frank Gillman.

With Pete Murray (Himself), Wendy Padbury (Carol), David Selwyn (Harold), Brian Burdon (Window Cleaner).

10.12.1967 19:25 – 19:55 **She's Your Mother – Not Mine** J
Written by Jimmy Grafton and Jeremy Lloyd; designed by Sylva Nadolny.

With Lionel Murton (Jack Meadows), Fabia Drake (Jane's Mother).

17.12.1967 19:25 – 19:55 **The Politician** J
Alternative transmissions: 21.02.1968: Rediffusion Television.
Written by Jimmy Grafton and Jeremy Lloyd; designed by David Catley.

With Lionel Murton (Jack Meadows), Arthur Mullard (Flunkey), David Kelsey (Vivian Drummond), Jeffrey Gardiner (Nigel Batley), Denis Handby (Dinner Organiser), Charles West (Psychiatrist).

31.12.1967 19:25 – 19:55 **The Security Leak** J
Written by Jimmy Grafton and Jeremy Lloyd; designed by David Catley.

With Lionel Murton (Jack Meadows), Brian Burdon (Kenny Miller), Bertie Hare (Hotel Manager), Dickie Martyn (Ice Cream Attendant), Anthony Kemp (Tommy), John Moulder-Brown (Arthur).

07.01.1968	**A Starlet is Born**	J

Alt.Title(s): *A Star Is Born*
Written by Jimmy Grafton and Jeremy Lloyd; designed by Barbara Bates.

With Lionel Murton (Jack Meadows), Peter Haigh, Sheila Steafel, Beatrix Mackey, Tom Gill.

14.01.1968	**Cold Comfort**	J

Written by Jimmy Grafton and Jeremy Lloyd; designed by David Catley.

With Lionel Murton, David Kelsey, Peter Graves, Len Lowe.

| 21.01.1968 | **The Amateur Professional** | J |

Alt.Title(s): *The Amateur Pro*

Written by Peter Myers, Jimmy Grafton and Jeremy Lloyd; designed by David Catley.

With Lionel Murton, Hugh Latimer, Vivienna Martin, Edwin Finn, Damaris Hayman, Josephine Gordon, Robert Perceval, Margaret Heald, Jayne Peach, Carole James, Janet Krasowski, Loraine Bertorelli.

| 28.01.1968 | **The Question of Wives** | J |

Alternative transmissions: 28.02.1968: Rediffusion Television.

Written by Jimmy Grafton and Jeremy Lloyd; designed by David Catley.

With Lionel Murton, Peter Graves, Jacqueline Jones, Hazel Graham, Sheena Marshe, Robert Scott Webber.

| 04.02.1968 | **Be a Clown** | J |

Alternative transmissions: 14.02.1968: Rediffusion Television.

Written by Jimmy Grafton and Jeremy Lloyd; designed by David Catley.

With Roger Avon, Johnnie Clayton, Len Lowe, Ali Hassan, Marika Rivera, George Claydon, Steven Follett, Ruben Martin and his Troupe.

| 11.02.1968 | **It's My Camera – Not Yours** | DB-R1 |

Written by Jimmy Grafton and Jeremy Lloyd; designed by David Catley.

With Lionel Murton, Hugh Latimer, Lizbeth Webb, Rita Webb, John East, David Rowlands.

Held by TDA/Kaleidoscope.

| 18.02.1968 | **The Mixed-Up Foursome** | J |

Written by Jimmy Grafton and Jeremy Lloyd; designed by David Catley.

With Lionel Murton, Henry Cotton, Eleanor Summerfield.

Most of these episodes were at least a year old when they were shown. The recording dates vary from 11.11.66 (for SS/45/11) to 10.02.67 (for SS/6/10). We suppose it is also slightly interesting that by this time the production numbers suggest it was made under the Series and Serials (SS) banner rather than Light Entertainment (LE) as in earlier seasons. This may be less a comment on this show and more a reflection on the changing career of Bill Hitchcock – who by this point was generally directing on drama series such as RAT CATCHERS and NO HIDING PLACE rather than the comedies and light entertainment programmes he had worked on earlier in his career. June Laverick retired from show business – at least for several years – in the mid 1960s following her second marriage. Despite being half his age at the time, the character Isla Blair plays in this final series – Jane Henderson – is supposed to be Dickie's wife. We are unsure whether it was explained on screen what had happened to the character's first wife.

THE DICKIE HENDERSON SHOW

An LWT production. Transmission details are for the ATV midlands region. Duration: 52 minutes.

Programme credit(s):   Written by Jimmy Grafton and Jeremy Lloyd; designed by Bill McPherson; executive producer Terry Henebery; produced and directed by Philip Casson.

Programme performer(s):   Dickie Henderson (Host), Lionel Blair and his Dancers (Resident dancers), Teddy Peiro.

	Holding / Source
13.03.1971	D2 / 2"

With Harry Secombe, Frank Gorshin.

| 20.03.1971 | D2 / 2" |

With Patrick Cargill, Sue Lloyd, Astrud Gilberto, Ronnie Carroll, Los Reales Del Paraguay.

| 27.03.1971 | D2 / 62 |

With Frank Gorshin, Dora Bryan, Clive Dunn, Roger Whittaker.

| 03.04.1971 | D2 / 2" |

With Roy Castle, Johnny Matthis, Dilys Watling, William Franklyn.

| 10.04.1971 | D2 / 2" |

With Sandie Shaw, David & Marianne Dalmour, June Whitfield, Ivor Emmanuel.

22.04.1971   D2 / 2"
With Noel Harrison, June Bronhill, Kenneth McKellar, Veronica Clifford.

06.05.1971   D2 / 2"
With Shirley Bassey, Terry-Thomas, Howard Keel.

THE EAMONN ANDREWS SHOW

An ABC/Thames production.

Programme performer(s):   Eamonn Andrews (Host).

SERIES 5

A Thames Television production. Transmission details are for the ATV midlands region. Duration: 40 minutes.
Season credit(s):   Produced by Bryan Izzard.

                                                        Holding / Source

26.12.1968 23:00 – 23:45 **Boxing Day Special: Royal Lancaster Hotel**   J / 40
With Kenny Ball (Interviewee), Danny La Rue (Interviewee), Roy Hudd (Interviewee), Dickie Henderson (Interviewee).

FACE THE MUSIC

A BBC production. Transmission details are for BBC Television.

Programme credit(s):   Production by Graeme Muir.

Programme performer(s):   Henry Hall (Host).

SERIES 1

Season credit(s):   Music associate Albert Marland; music arranged by Albert Marland; orchestra directed by Henry Hall and Eric Robinson.

                                                        Holding / Source

17.01.1953 21:05 – 22:05   NR / Live
Dance direction by George Carden; settings by Michael Yates.

With Bernard Miles, Line Renaud, Harry S. Pepper, Dickie Henderson [as Dickie Henderson, Junior], Benjamin Frankel, The George Carden Dancers, The Peter Knight Singers, The Original BBC Dance Orchestra.

FALL IN, THE STARS

An Independent Television production for LWT. Transmission details are for the ATV midlands region. Duration: 80 minutes.

Television presentation by Jon Scoffield; produced by William Chappell.

Maria Aitken, Moira Anderson, The Beverley Sisters, Georgia Brown, Gemma Craven, Charlie Drake, Arthur English, Sir John Gielgud, Anita Harris, Penelope Keith, Koffee 'N' Kreme, Mrs Mills, Johnnie Ray, Dickie Henderson, Jimmy Jewel, Dame Vera Lynn, Sir John Mills, Beryl Reid, André Prokovsky, Galina Samsova, Harry Secombe, Simone, Tommy Trinder, Joan Turner, Denis Walter, June Whitfield, Elaine Bird, Paul Eddington, Christopher Gable, Henry McGee, The London Palladium Orchestra, The Cliff Adams Singers, Samantha Stevens Dancers.

                                                        Holding / Source

15.05.1977   DB / 2"

FOR LOVE OR MONEY

An ABC Midlands production for ABC. Transmission details are for the ABC midlands region. Duration: 25 minutes.

The show in which contestants can win from £s to pennies or take away wonderful prizes.

SERIES 1

	Holding / Source
03.01.1960	J / 40

Directed by Marjory Ruse.
With Dickie Henderson (Host).

10.01.1960	J / 40

Directed by Marjory Ruse.
With Dickie Henderson (Host).

17.01.1960	J / 40

Directed by Marjory Ruse.
With Dickie Henderson (Host).

24.01.1960	J / 40

Directed by Marjory Ruse.
With Dickie Henderson (Host), Ann Parson.

According to The Stage and Television Today, the hosts at the beginning were Jewel and Warriss. A strike affecting TV Times production during the summer of 1959 has, so far, prevented us from verifying this, and from determining for how many weeks this was the case.

Although later editions were taped, it may be that the earlier ones were broadcast live and never recorded.

A FUNNY THING... FOR NEW YEAR

A BBC production for BBC 1. Transmission details are for BBC 1.

Memories and anecdotes from stars with a lifetime in show business.

Programme credit(s):   Production by John Longley.

	Holding / Source
06.11.1973 15:00 – 15:05	J / 2"

With Dickie Henderson.

07.11.1973 14:55 – 15:00	J / 2"

With Dickie Henderson.

09.11.1973 15:55 – 16:00	J / 2"

With Dickie Henderson.

BBC have a recording spool for the Arthur Askey editions from 11, 12 and 14 Sept 1973, and complete editions of Jimmy Edwards from 18, 19 and 21 September 1973.

GREEN ROOM CAVALCADE (RADIO)

A BBC production for BBC Home Service. Transmission details are for BBC Home Service.

Some of the stars who appeared in the midnight show at the London Coliseum.

Daphne Anderson, Denis Bowen, Jane Baxter, Edith Evans, Gwen Ffrangcon-Davies, John Gielgud, Frankie Howerd, Dickie Henderson, John Justin, Vivien Leigh, Eve Lister, Arthur Macrae, Laurence Olivier, Nigel Patrick, Ralph Richardson, Tommy Trinder, Bruce Trent.

	Holding / Source
27.03.1956 20:00 – 21:00	J / AA

THE HARRY SECOMBE SHOW

A BBC production for BBC 1. Transmission details are for BBC 1.

Programme performer(s):   Harry Secombe (Host).

SERIES 3

Duration: 45 minutes.

Season credit(s):   Programme associate Jimmy Grafton; orchestra directed by Peter Knight; production by Terry Hughes.

Holding / Source

16.10.1971 20:00 – 20:45   HD-R1 / 2"

Designed by Bernard Lloyd-Jones and Brian Tregidden.

With Dickie Henderson, Kenneth McKellar, Kiri Te Kanawa, Vicky Leandros, Julian Orchard.

HAVE A MERRY EVERYTHING (RADIO)

A BBC production for BBC Light Programme. Transmission details are for BBC Light Programme.

Dickie Henderson plays a few records to match your midday mood.

Dickie Henderson.

Holding / Source

25.12.1965 12:00 – 12:31   J / AA

HERE'S TO THE NEXT TIME

A BBC production. Transmission details are for BBC Television. Usual duration: 45 minutes.

Programme performer(s):   Henry Hall and his Orchestra.

Holding / Source

09.05.1959 19:30 – 20:30   J

Duration: 60 minutes.

Introduced by John Snagge; music arranged by Alan Bristow; dance direction by Joan Davis; designed by George Djurkovic; production by Russell Turner.

With Cliff Richard and The Drifters, Joan Regan, Dickie Valentine, Lucille Graham, Mike Hall, The Joan Davis Dancers, The Mike Sammes Singers, Arthur Askey, Dickie Henderson, Anthea Askey.

HOGMANAY [GRAMPIAN]

A Grampian Television production. Transmission details are for the Grampian Television region.

Holding / Source

31.12.1971   **Dickie Henderson's Hogmanay**   J

With Dickie Henderson (Host).

HUSBAND OF THE YEAR

A Yorkshire Television production. Transmission details are for the Yorkshire Television region.

In search of the ideal husband.

Programme credit(s):   Devised by Brad Ashton.

SERIES 2

Duration: 25 minutes.

Season credit(s):   Written by Brad Ashton; research Shirley Taylor; designed by Richard Jarvis; produced by Terry Henebery; directed by David Millard.

Season cast: With Pete Murray (Chairman), Marjorie Proops (Panellist), Leslie Randall (Panellist).

Holding / Source

24.08.1976 19:05 – 19:35 **The Grand Final**   J / 2"

With Beryl Reid (Jury), Dickie Henderson (Jury), Tricia Murray (Jury), Terry Wadkin (Jury).

I WISH I'D SAID THAT

A Polo Productions production. Untransmitted. Duration: 24 minutes.

Written by Barry Cryer; music by John Patrick; designed by Anna Ridley; produced and directed by Paul Stewart Laing.

Dickie Henderson (Host), Kenneth Williams, Peter Goodwright, Johnny More, Karen Kay [as Karen Kaye], Lionel Murton.

Holding / Source

##.##.####   **Untransmitted Pilot**   DV / 1"

IF THEY LIKED YOU THEY LET YOU LIVE (RADIO)

A BBC Manchester production for BBC Radio 4. Transmission details are for BBC Radio 4. Duration: 45 minutes.

Tales of death and disaster from the 'graveyard of the English comedian', the infamous Empire Theatre, Glasgow.

Presented by Tony Bilbow; production by Peter Everett.

Duggie Brown, Eric Morecambe, Ted Ray [in Archive Material], Tommy Trinder, Harry Worth, Arthur Askey, Dickie Henderson, Roy Castle, Des O'Connor.

Holding / Source

17.08.1980 22:15 – 23:00   DA / AA

"I'M BOB – HE'S DICKIE"

An ATV production. Transmission details are for the ATV midlands region. Usual duration: 50 minutes.

Programme performer(s):   Bob Monkhouse (Host), Dickie Henderson (Host).

Holding / Source

06.07.1977   DB / 2"

Written by Dick Vosburgh and Garry Chambers; musical director Jack Parnell; choreography by Paddy Stone; designed by Michael Bailey; produced and directed by Paul Stewart Laing.

With Michele Dotrice, Kate Williams, Koffee 'N' Kreme, Felicity Harrison, The Paddy Stone Dancers, The Brownies, Jack Parnell and his Orchestra, Blake Butler.

The script also credits Eddie Braben as a writer.

##.##.####   **Unedited Studio Recording from Programme 1**   UM / 2"

Duration: 20 minutes.

01.02.1978   DB / 2"

Written by Bob Monkhouse, Dick Vosburgh and Garry Chambers; musical director Jack Parnell; choreography by Irving Davies; designed by Richard Plumb; produced and directed by Paul Stewart Laing.

With Una Stubbs, Sylvia Syms, Clodagh Rodgers, The Irving Davies Dancers, Jack Parnell and his Orchestra, The Brownies.

06.09.1978   DB / 2"

Written by Bob Monkhouse, Dick Vosburgh and Garry Chambers; musical director Jack Parnell; choreography by Irving Davies; designed by Michael Bailey and Richard Plumb; produced and directed by Paul Stewart Laing.

With The Hudson Brothers, Janet Brown, The Irving Davies Dancers, Jack Parnell and his Orchestra, The Brownies, Patrick French, Steve Kelly.

I'M DICKIE--THAT'S SHOWBUSINESS

An ATV production. Transmission details are for the ATV midlands region. Duration: 50 minutes.

Written by Garry Chambers; music by Jack Parnell and his Orchestra; designed by Tony Ferris; produced and directed by Paul Stewart Laing.

Dickie Henderson (Host), Vince Hill, Helen Gelzer, Prunella Scales, The Clark Brothers, Roy Budd, The Minitones, The Irving Davies Dancers.

                                                                                              Holding / Source
04.10.1978   DB / 2"

With Vince Hill, Prunella Scales, Roy Budd.

INTERNATIONAL CABARET

A BBC production for BBC 2. Transmission details are for BBC 2.

SERIES 4: from The Talk of the Town
Duration: 40 minutes.
Season performer(s): With The Young Generation.

                                                                                              Holding / Source
03.01.1969   J / 2"

Produced and directed by G. B. Lupino.

With Les Dawson (Presenter), Dickie Henderson, Jackie Trent and Tony Hatch, Silvan.

INTERNATIONAL PRO-CELEBRITY GOLF

A BBC production for BBC 2. Transmission details are for BBC 2. Usual duration: 50 minutes.

Mixed teams of professional golfers and enthusiastic show-business amateurs from America and Britain compete.

SERIES 2
Season credit(s):   Introduced by Henry Longhurst; commentary by Peter Alliss; television presentation by Richard Tilling, Fred Viner and Huw Jones; produced by A. P. Wilkinson.

Season performer(s): With Peter Oosterhaus (Professional (UK)), Tom Weiskopf (Professional (USA)).

                                                                                              Holding / Source
02.03.1976 20:10 – 21:00 **Match 8**   DB-D3 / 2"

With Dickie Henderson, Dick Martin.

SERIES 6: The Marley Trophy
Season credit(s):   Commentary by Peter Alliss; television presentation by Richard Tilling and Alastair
                      Scott; produced by David Kenning.
Season performer(s): With Lee Trevino, Ben Crenshaw.

Holding / Source

25.01.1980 21:25 – 22:15 **Match 4**   DB-D3 / 2"
With Dickie Henderson, Glyn Houston.

IT'S A FUNNY BUSINESS (RADIO)

A BBC Manchester production for BBC Radio 2. Transmission details are for BBC Radio 2.

Celebrities relive memorable moments from their careers.

SERIES 4
Season credit(s):   Presented by Mike Craig; production by Mike Craig.

Holding / Source

18.12.1980 22:02 – 22:30   / AA
With Dickie Henderson.

JACK HYLTON PRESENTS...

A Jack Hylton TV Productions production for Associated-Rediffusion. Transmission details are for Associated-Rediffusion. Usual duration: 50 minutes.

An umbrella title for occasional comedy and variety specials.

Holding / Source

13.10.1955   J
Duration: 50 minutes.
Directed by Kenneth Carter.

With David Nixon, The Tiller Girls, Roger Carne, Dickie Henderson, Lane and Truzzi, Shirley Bassey, Dorothy Squires, Naughton and Gold, Morton Fraser and his Harmonica Gang, Rossano Brazzi.

Miriam Karlin, Frank Cook, Ken Wilson, Hermione Gingold and Henry Kendall, Paddy Larner and Peter Grant, and The Merry Martins were billed in TV Times but, apparently, did not appear. David Nixon, Roger Garne, Morton Fraser and his Harmonica Gang and Rossano Brazzi were not billed in TV Times but, apparently, did appear.

21.12.1956 20:30 – 21:00 **Christmas Greetings**   J
Duration: 25 minutes.
A half-hour of light-hearted, seasonal entertainment.
Directed by Peter Croft.
With Dickie Henderson, Rosalina Neri, Phillipe Clay, The Peiro Brothers.

29.12.1958 21:30 – 22:00 **Highlights of 1958**   J
Duration: 25 minutes.
Excerpts from top shows.
Directed by Bill Hitchcock.

With Anne Shelton (Presenter), Jack Hylton (Presenter), Arthur Askey, Colette Brosset, Robert Dhéry, Hughie Green, Dickie Henderson, Richard Murdoch.

THE JACK JACKSON SHOW

An ATV production. Transmission details are for the ATV midlands region. Duration: 25 minutes.

Programme credit(s):   Devised by Jack Jackson and Mark White.

Programme performer(s):   Jack Jackson (Host).

SERIES 4

Transmission details are for the ATV midlands region.

Season credit(s):   Programme editor Mark White.

	Holding / Source
01.04.1959 23:00 – 23:30	J / Live40

Designed by Raymond White; produced by Peter Glover.

With Dickie Henderson, Glen Mason, Malcolm Jackson, Paddy Edwards, Pamela Manson.

THE JACK JONES SHOW

A BBC production for BBC 2. Transmission details are for BBC 2. Usual duration: 45 minutes.

Programme performer(s):   Jack Jones (Host).

SERIES 1

Season credit(s):   Musical directors Joe Kloess and Derek Warne; choreography by Flick Colby; production by Stanley Dorfman.

Season performer(s):   With The Ladybirds, Pan's People.

	Holding / Source
03.02.1974 20:15 – 21:00	DB-D3 / 2"

Designed by Lesley Joan Bremness.

With Dickie Henderson, Lynsey De Paul.

THE KEN DODD SHOW

A BBC production for BBC 1. Transmission details are for BBC 1.

Programme performer(s):   Ken Dodd (Host).

SERIES 4

Duration: 45 minutes.

Season credit(s):   Written by Eddie Braben and Ken Dodd; choreography by Miss Bluebell; produced and directed by Duncan Wood.

Season performer(s):   With Roger Stevenson, The Diddymen, The Bluebell Girls.

	Holding / Source
07.08.1966	J

Designed by Melvyn Cornish.

With Dickie Henderson, Hope and Keen, Judy Collins, Jack Douglas, Graham Stark, The Augmented N.D.O..

Allegedly live from Blackpool!

LATE NIGHT EXTRA (RADIO)

A BBC production for BBC Radio 2. Transmission details are for BBC Radio 2.

	Holding / Source
03.01.1973 22:02 – 00:00	J / Live

Duration: 118 minutes.

Production by Tony Luke.

With Simon Bates (Host), Chico Arnez, Dickie Henderson, The Laurie Holloway Trio.

LAUGHTER IN THE AIR (RADIO)

A BBC production for BBC Radio 2. Transmission details are for BBC Radio 2.

The story of radio comedy in eleven parts.

Holding / Source

02.01.1979 22:02 – 23:02 **The Cat's Whiskers**   DA / AA

Dickie Henderson invites you to fiddle with your Crystal and top up your accumulator.

Presented by Dickie Henderson; written by Denis Gifford; production by Bobby Jaye.

With Claude Dampier and Billie Carlyle [in Archive Material], Gillie Potter [in Archive Material], Leonard Henry [in Archive Material], Leslie Sarony [in Archive Material], Clapham and Dwyer [in Archive Material], Murgatroyd and Winterbottom [in Archive Material], The Western Brothers [in Archive Material].

09.01.1979 22:02 – 23:02 **Ladies and Gentlemen – Music Hall**   DA / AA

Dickie Henderson invites you to tune in your superheterodyne receiver.

Presented by Dickie Henderson; written by Denis Gifford; production by Bobby Jaye.

With Arthur Askey [in Archive Material], Elsie and Doris Waters [in Archive Material], Sandy Powell [in Archive Material], Kenway and Young [in Archive Material], Charles Shadwell [in Archive Material].

16.01.1979 22:02 – 23:02 **Hello Playmates, It's That Man Again**   DA / AA

Dickie Henderson invites you to take a trip on the 'Band Wagon' once more and then rejoin some of those wild and wonderful characters that made ITMA what it was. And still is.

Presented by Dickie Henderson; compiled by Frank Morgan; written by Frank Morgan; production by Martin Fisher.

With Arthur Askey [in Archive Material], Richard Murdoch [in Archive Material], Tommy Handley [in Archive Material], Maurice Denham [in Archive Material], Deryck Guyler [in Archive Material], Molly Weir [in Archive Material].

23.01.1979 22:02 – 23:02 **Shows, Comical, Servicemen for the Use Of!**   DA / AA

Dickle Henderson invites you to try on your battle dress for size: get some sand back into your turn-ups; 'Stand Easy' at 'Waterlogged Spa' and Much Binding in the Marsh, and other wartime shows that kept people going in the blackout and beyond.

Presented by Dickie Henderson; compiled by Frank Morgan; written by Frank Morgan; production by Martin Fisher.

30.01.1979 22:02 – 23:02 **Pardon Me, Your Sitcom's Showing!**   DA / AA

Dickie Henderson invites you to retread the path of radio situation comedy.

Presented by Dickie Henderson; compiled by Frank Morgan; written by Frank Morgan; production by Martin Fisher.

With Leslie Phillips [in Archive Material], Ben Lyon [in Archive Material], Eric Barker [in Archive Material], George Cole [in Archive Material], Jon Pertwee [in Archive Material].

For the first four weeks the series was billed in Radio Times as consisting of ten parts.

THE LESLIE CROWTHER SHOW

An LWT production. Transmission details are for the ATV midlands region. Duration: 52 minutes.

Programme credit(s):   Written by Peter Dulay and Spike Mullins; additional material by Dick Vosburgh; musical director Harry Rabinowitz; designed by Bryce Walmsley; executive producer Terry Henebery; produced and directed by William G. Stewart.

Programme performer(s): Leslie Crowther (Host).

Holding / Source

27.02.1971   J / 2"

Alternative transmissions: 13.02.1971 19:15 – 20:15: LWT.

With Dickie Henderson, Nina, Luis Alberto del Parana, Sheila Bernette, Aleta Morrison, Albert Modley, Chic Murray, Rostal and Schaefer [as Peter Rostal and Paul Schaefer].

LONDON NIGHT OUT

A Thames Television production. Transmission details are for the ATV/Central region. Usual duration: 52 minutes.

Programme performer(s):   Tom O'Connor (Host).

SERIES 2

Transmission details are for the ATV midlands region.

Season credit(s):   Script consultant Dick Hills; musical director Alan Braden; choreography by Irving Davies; produced by Paul Stewart Laing.

Season performer(s): With The Ladybirds (Backing Vocals), The Irving Davies Dancers (Resident Dancers).

Holding / Source

28.11.1979 20:00 – 21:00   DB-D3 / 2"

Directed by Paul Stewart Laing.

With Dickie Henderson, Gerard Kenny, Johnny Hutch and The Halfwits, Geraldine.

THE LONDON PALLADIUM SHOW

An ATV London production for ATV. Transmission details are for the ABC midlands region. Duration: 50 minutes.

SERIES 2

Season performer(s): With Jack Parnell and his Orchestra, The Michael Sammes Singers.

Holding / Source

06.11.1966   R1 / 40

Designed by Bill McPherson; executive producer Bill Ward; associate producer Albert Locke; directed by Albert Locke and Colin Clews.

With Fess Parker, Rudolf Nureyev & Svetlana Beriosova, Dickie Henderson, The Seekers, Dave Allen, Millicent Martin, The Bronsky Twins.

Recorded 05.06.1966.

NB: Albert Locke directed the colour recording, Colin Clews the monochrome one.

Held at New York Public Library and by Kaleidoscope.

SERIES 3

Holding / Source

10.03.1968   J / Live

Designed by Eric Shedden; produced by Colin Clews.

With Dickie Henderson (Compere), Tony Bennett, Buddy Rich and his Orchestra, Dusty Springfield, Les Dawson, Les Farfadets, Jack Parnell and his Orchestra.

LOOK WHO'S TALKING

A Border Television production. Transmission details are for border region. Usual duration: 25 minutes.

Programme credit(s):   Produced by Derek Batey.

Programme performer(s):   Derek Batey (Presenter).

SERIES 4

Season credit(s):   Designed by John Henderson.

	Holding / Source
24.12.1974	B / 2"

Duration: 50 minutes.

Alternative transmissions: 24.12.1974 13:45 – 14:45: ATV.

In this special festive edition, Derek Batey introduces again some of the stars he has met during the last year - including Arthur Askey, Dickie Henderson, Ted Ray, Norman Collier, Anita Harris, Ray Alan and Lord Charles, Peter Goodwright, Kenneth McKellar, Allan Stewart, Tessie O'Shea, Reginald Bosanquet, Frank Carson, Sandy Powell, Chick Murray, Jimmy Logan, Johnny More, Roger Whittaker, Tony Hatch and Jackie Trent.

Directed by Norman Fraser.

With Arthur Askey, Dickie Henderson, Ted Ray, Norman Collier, Anita Harris, Ray Alan and Lord Charles, Peter Goodwright, Kenneth McKellar, Allan Stewart, Tessie O'Shea, Reginald Bosanquet, Frank Carson, Sandy Powell, Chic Murray, Jimmy Logan, Johnny More, Roger Whittaker, Tony Hatch, Jackie Trent.

Derek Batey introduces clips from the earlier series.

Most of this season looks to have been shown around the ITV network on the same day as the Border transmissions, but with most regions taking it at lunchtime and only Border giving it an evening slot.

Transmission details are for the Central region.

	Holding / Source
##.##.####	B / 2"

With Dickie Henderson.

	Holding / Source
##.##.####	B / 2"

With Dickie Henderson.

The dates by which the surviving material has been documented do not match broadcast dates, so we have assumed – until we learn anything to the contrary – that these are recording dates. Some of these may well be among the programmes listed above but until we have a full listing or further information – given that a number of guests appear more than once – it's not possible for us to apportion these across the series.

See also: THEY SAID THIS?

LOOKS FAMILIAR

A Thames Television production. Transmission details are for the ATV midlands region. Usual duration: 25 minutes.

Programme credit(s):   Devised by Denis Gifford.

Programme performer(s):   Denis Norden (Presenter).

SERIES 2

Season credit(s):   Produced by David Clark; directed by Anthony Parker.

	Holding / Source
20.06.1973 14:55 – 15:25	DB / 2"

Research John Pullen-Burry.

With Danny La Rue, Diana Dors, Dickie Henderson.

	Holding / Source
03.09.1973 14:00 – 14:30	DB / 2"

Research John Pullen-Burry.

With Danny La Rue, Diana Dors, Dickie Henderson.

SERIES 5
Season credit(s):   Research Colin Williams; designed by Rod Stratfold; produced by David Clark.

Holding / Source

19.11.1975 15:25 – 15:55   DB-D3 / 2"
Alternative transmissions: 08.03.1976 22:30 – 23:00: Thames Television.
Directed by Daphne Shadwell.
With Sammy Cahn, Anne Shelton, Dickie Henderson, Benny Green.

SERIES 9
Season credit(s):   Research Colin Williams; designed by Alison Waugh; produced and directed by David
                      Clark.

Holding / Source

13.03.1980 15:45 – 16:15   DB / 2"
With Dickie Henderson, Liz Fraser, Brian Johnston.

SERIES 12
Duration: 40 minutes.
Season credit(s):   Associate producer Colin Williams; produced and directed by David Clark.

Holding / Source

06.09.1984   1" / 1"
With Ivy Benson, Dickie Henderson, George Meaton, Ronnie Ronalde.

LULU

A BBC production for BBC 1. Transmission details are for BBC 1.
Programme performer(s):   Lulu.

SERIES 2
Duration: 45 minutes.
Season credit(s):   Written by Eric Davidson; choreography by Nigel Lythgoe; produced by Stewart Morris.
Season performer(s): With Segment, The Nigel Lythgoe Dancers, Alyn Ainsworth and his Orchestra.

Holding / Source

05.04.1975   DB-D3 / 2"
Designed by Brian Tregidden and Robin Tarsnane; directed by Stanley Appel.
With Dickie Henderson, Basil Brush, Bernie Clifton, Rostal and Schaefer.

THE MAIN ATTRACTION

A BBC production for BBC 1. Transmission details are for BBC 1. Usual duration: 40 minutes.

SERIES 1
Season credit(s):   Produced by John Fisher.

Holding / Source

13.08.1983   DB / 2"
With Sammy Cahn, Gemma Craven, Dickie Henderson, Mr Acker Bilk and his Paramount Jazz Band, Ricky
Jay, Janet Brown.

MAINLY MILLICENT

An ATV production. Transmission details are for the ATV midlands region.

Programme performer(s): Millicent Martin (Host).

SERIES 2

Transmission details are for the ATV London region. Duration: 30 minutes.

Season credit(s):   Written by John Warren and John Singer; choreography by Paddy Stone; designed by Bill McPherson; produced and directed by Francis Essex.

Season performer(s): With The Jack Parnell Band, Raymond Dalziel, Fred Evans, Ian Kaye, David Kerr, Geoffrey L'Cise, Vince Logan, Fred Peters, David Wright.

Holding / Source

22.05.1965   R1 / 40

With Dickie Henderson.

MALCOLM MITCHELL

A BBC production. Transmission details are for BBC Television.

A programme of music, song and light conversation.

Programme performer(s): Malcolm Mitchell (Host), The Malcolm Mitchell Trio.

SERIES 2

Season credit(s):   Devised by Richard Afton; designed by Barry Newbery; production by Richard Afton.

Season performer(s): With Arthur Jones, Diana Noble.

Holding / Source

25.09.1960 14:25 – 15:00   J / 40

With Dickie Henderson, Raymond, Sylvia Sands, Bobby Shipman, Carole Hickey, Hugh Lloyd.

MERELY MELVILLE (RADIO)

A BBC production for BBC Radio 4. Transmission details are for BBC Radio 4. Duration: 28 minutes.

A tribute to the late Alan Melville, the great master of intimate revue.

Introduced by Ian Carmichael; written by John Preston; research John Preston; production by Andy Aliffe.

Dame Anna Neagle (Interviewee), Hermione Gingold (Interviewee), Dora Bryan (Interviewee), Hermione Baddeley (Interviewee), Beryl Reid (Interviewee), Dulcie Gray (Interviewee), Dickie Henderson (Interviewee).

Holding / Source

19.04.1984 12:27 – 12:55   AA / AAS

MIDDAY MUSIC-HALL (RADIO)

Commissioned by BBC Radio various. Transmission details are for BBC Radio various.

Commissioned by BBC Home Service. Transmission details are for BBC Home Service.

Holding / Source

11.04.1955 12:20 – 12:55 **Bank Holiday Music-Hall**   NR / Live

Orchestra conducted by Paul Fenoulhet.

With Dickie Henderson (Compere), The Coronets, Brent Davies, Pat Gilbert, Kenny Baker, Louise Traill, Leon Cortez, Augmented BBC Variety Orchestra.

MOIRA ANDERSON SINGS

A BBC Scotland production for BBC 1. Transmission details are for BBC 1. Duration: 25 minutes.

Programme performer(s):   Moira Anderson (Herself).

SERIES 3

Season credit(s):   Produced and directed by James Moir.

Season performer(s): With BBC Scottish Radio Orchestra.

Holding / Source

19.05.1969   J

Written by Jack Gerson; designed by David McKenzie.

With Dickie Henderson.

THE MUSIC SHOP

Alternative/Working Title(s): ABC MUSIC SHOP / ATV MUSIC SHOP

An ATV London production. Transmission details are for the ATV midlands region. Duration: 25 minutes.

SERIES 4

Transmission details are for the ATV London region.

Holding / Source

03.05.1959 14:55 – 15:25 **Programme 34**   J / Live

Designed by Pembroke Duttson; production by Dicky Leeman.

With Dickie Henderson, Marino Marini and his Quartet, Mike and Bernie Winters, Mary Nolan, Jack Parnell and The Counter-Hands.

TV Times credits for the majority of series 4 carried the line 'Sets designed by Jon Scoffield' but the design department schedules indicated that a number of other ATV designers worked on the series. All designers' names, apart from Scoffield's have come from those schedules.

MUSIC-HALL (RADIO)

A BBC production for BBC Home Service. Transmission details are for BBC Home Service.

Holding / Source

15.05.1948 20:00 – 21:00   J / AA

Announcer Denys Drower; orchestra conducted by Rae Jenkins; production by John Sharman.

With Dickie Henderson [as Dick Henderson Jnr], The Doyle Kids, Jim and Dan Sherry, Max Wall, Peter Dawson, Revnell and West, BBC Variety Orchestra.

MY WILDEST DREAM

A Granada production. Transmission details are for the Granada region. Duration: 25 minutes.

Holding / Source

26.12.1956 21:30 – 22:00   J / R1

With Kenneth MacLeod (Chairman), Tommy Trinder, David Nixon, Alfred Marks, Dickie Henderson.

02.01.1957 22:15 – 22:45   J / R1

With Kenneth MacLeod (Chairman), Tommy Trinder, David Nixon, Alfred Marks, Dickie Henderson, Anton Diffring.

09.01.1957 22:15 – 22:45   J / R1

With Kenneth MacLeod (Chairman), Tommy Trinder, David Nixon, Alfred Marks, Dickie Henderson.

16.01.1957 22:15 – 22:45   J / R1

With Kenneth MacLeod (Chairman), Tommy Trinder, David Nixon, Alfred Marks, Dickie Henderson.

A NATIONAL SALUTE TO THE FALKLANDS TASK FORCE

An LWT production for ITV. Transmission details are for the Central region.

Programme credit(s):   Introduced by Michael Nicholson; devised by Robert Nesbitt; staged by Robert Nesbitt; produced by David Bell; directed by Alan Boyd.

Programme performer(s):   Adam Ant, Michael Aspel, Ronnie Corbett, Leslie Crowther, Billy Dainty, Paul Daniels, Les Dawson, Wayne Eagling, Jill Gascoine, Anita Harris, Dickie Henderson, Danny La Rue, Vera Lynn, Virginia McKenna, Alfred Marks, Peter Morrison, Merle Park, Harry Secombe, Alvin Stardust, Tommy Steele, Jimmy Tarbuck, Kim Wilde, Laurence Olivier, Band of the Household Cavalry, National Theatre, Royal Shakespeare Company, English National Opera, The Royal Ballet, Band of the 2nd Battalion Parachute Regiment.

	Holding / Source
18.07.1982 19:45 – 21:00 **Part One** Duration: 65 minutes.	D2 / LivePAL
18.07.1982 21:25 – 23:00 **Part Two** Duration: 80 minutes.	D2 / LivePAL

The ITN News was transmitted in the intermission.

NIGHT OF 100 STARS

An LWT production. Transmission details are for the ATV midlands region. Duration: 145 minutes.

In the presence of Princess Margaret, Terry Wogan introduces the stars.

Written by Ken Hoare, Garry Chambers, Colin Bostock-Smith, Eric Merriman and Sid Green; dances staged by Robert Nesbitt; choreography by Irving Davies and Brian Rogers; designed by Bill McPherson; produced by David Bell and Richard Drewett; directed by Alan Boyd.

Terry Wogan (Host), Marti Webb, Susannah York, Bruce Forsyth, Ron Moody, Wayne Sleep, Honor Blackman, Edward Fox, Mary Malcolm, Dickie Henderson, Alfie Bass, Ian Lavender, Charles West, Stella Moray, Jess Conrad, Rosamund Shelley, John Diedrich, Caroline Villiers, Cannon and Ball, Berni Flint, Dave Wolfe, Jimmy Cricket, Hinge & Bracket, Dudley Stevens, Bernard Cribbins, Denis Quilley, Jill Gascoine, Peter Cook, David Essex, David Frost, William Rushton, Kenneth Cope, Lance Percival, Lulu, Robert Powell, Twiggy, Jean Marsh, Albert Finney, Christopher Lee, Sean Connery, James Mason, Susan George, Vera Lynn, Paul Schofield, Jessie Matthews, Margaret Lockwood, Stewart Granger, Joan Greenwood, Dulcie Gray, Michael Denison, Anna Neagle, Anthony Steel, Claire Bloom, Donald Sinden, Phyllis Calvert, Norman Wisdom, Richard Todd, Kenneth More, Dinah Sheridan, Diana Dors, Bryan Forbes, Nigel Patrick, Shirley Anne Field, Tom Courtenay, Jack Wild, Mark Lester, Oliver Reed, Simon Ward, Jenny Agutter, Graham Chapman, Hazel O'Connor, Phil Daniels, Petricia Rock, Julia McKenzie, Millicent Martin, Leslie Mitchell, Sylvia Peters, Barbara Kelly, Eamonn Andrews, Ruth Dunning, Edward Evans, Christopher Beeny, Peggy Mount, Harry Fowler, Bill Fraser, Dai Francis, John Boulter, Margaret Savage, George Mitchell, Hughie Green, David Jacobs, Alan Freeman, Don Lang, Pete Murray, Josephine Douglas, Bernie Winters, Joe Brown, Marty Wilde, Showaddywaddy, Elvi Hale, Annette Crosbie, Raymond Francis, Eric Lander, James Ellis, Terence Edmond, Joe Brady, Frank Windsor, Nyree Dawn Porter, Carol Drinkwater, Christopher Timothy, Susan Penhaligon, James Aubrey, Deborah Grant, Frank Finlay, Andrew Cruickshank, Bill Simpson, Rula Lenska, Charlotte Cornwell, Jack Hedley, Hans Meyer, Christopher Neame, Joan Benham, David Langton, Ian Ogilvy, Rachel Gurney, Simon Williams, Patsy Smart, Jenny Tomasin, Gordon Jackson, Dennis Waterman, George Cole, Lewis Collins, Martin Shaw, Derek Nimmo, George Layton, Geoffrey Davies, Ernest Clark, Jacqui Ann Carr, Carol Hawkins, Peter Cleall, Peter Denyer, Liz Gebhardt, Reg Varney, Anna Karen, Bob Grant, Doris Hare, Stephen Lewis, Richard O'Sullivan, Paula Wilcox, Tessa Wyatt, John Le Mesurier, Bill Pertwee, Arnold Ridley, Frank Williams, Ron Tarr, Alyn Ainsworth and his Orchestra.

	Holding / Source
21.12.1980 19:15 – 21:45	D2 / 2"

OFF THE RECORD

A BBC production. Transmission details are for BBC Television. Usual duration: 30 minutes.

Programme credit(s): Music conducted by Stanley Black; produced by James Gilbert.

Programme performer(s): Jack Payne (Host), The Concert Orchestra, The George Mitchell Singers.

SERIES 2

Season credit(s): Production by Bill Cotton Jnr.

Holding / Source

26.11.1956   J / Live

With Max Bygraves, Shirley Abicair, Dickie Henderson, Dorothy Squires, Ronnie Harris, The Victor Feldman Quartet.

ON STAGE (RADIO)

A BBC production for BBC Light Programme. Transmission details are for BBC Light Programme.

Holding / Source

05.08.1964 19:31 – 20:30 **Scarborough**   J / AA

Orchestra conducted by Bernard Herrmann; production by Geoff Lawrence.

With Dickie Henderson (Host), Arthur Haynes, Nicholas Parsons, Leslie Noyes, Joan Regan, Julius Nehring, Vince Hill, Hope and Keen, John Mitchell, Desmond Lane, BBC Northern Dance Orchestra.

From the Floral Hall, Scarborough.

PARADE

A BBC production. Transmission details are for BBC Television.

The show business magazine.

Programme credit(s): Orchestra directed by Harry Rabinowitz; designed by Malcolm Goulding; produced by Bryan Sears.

Programme performer(s): Alan Melville (Host).

Holding / Source

30.11.1960 20:50 – 21:30 **Programme 9**   J / Live

Choreography by Eleanor Fazan; assistant producer Brian Marber.

With Dickie Henderson, Kay Cavendish, Robert Harbin, Burda Cann (Dancer), Elaine Carr (Dancer), Ina Clare (Dancer), Sidonie Darrell (Dancer), Sheila Falconer (Dancer), Greta Hamby (Dancer).

PARKINSON

A BBC production for BBC 1. Transmission details are for BBC 1.

Programme performer(s): Michael Parkinson (Host).

SERIES 4

Duration: 60 minutes.

Season credit(s): Music by Harry Stoneham; produced by Roger Ordish.

Holding / Source

14.12.1974   DB-1" / 2"

Directed by Colin Strong.

With Dickie Henderson, Henry Mancini.

SERIES 10
Duration: 60 minutes.
Season credit(s):   Programme associate Chris Greenwood; music by Harry Stoneham; assistant
                     producers Graham Lindsay and Gill Stribling-Wright; produced by John Fisher; directed
                     by Bruce Milliard.

Holding / Source

24.09.1980 23:02 – 00:05   DB-D3 / 2"
With Lee Trevino, Bob Hope, Dickie Henderson, Olivia Newton-John.

PASSWORD

A BBC production for BBC Various, made in association with Goodson Todman Productions. Transmission
details are for BBC Various. Duration: 30 minutes.
Guest personalities help or hinder members of the public to gusss the password.
Programme credit(s):   Devised by Mark Goodson and Bill Todman; designed by Paul Montague;
                        produced by Cecil Korer.

SERIES 2
Commissioned by BBC 1. Transmission details are for BBC 1.
Season performer(s): With Eleanor Summerfield (Chairman).

Holding / Source

18.02.1974 15:30 – 16:00   J / 2"
Directed by Peggy Walker.
With Diane Hart, Dickie Henderson.

PLAY IT AGAIN

A Tyne Tees Television production. Transmission details are for the Central region. Duration: 25 minutes.
SERIES 5
Transmission details are for the Central region.
Season credit(s):   Research Christine Williams; designed by Eric Briers; produced by David Jones;
                     directed by Bernard Preston.
Season performer(s): With Tony Bilbow (Presenter).

Holding / Source

22.09.1982 15:45 – 16:15   J / 2"
With Dickie Henderson.

POP SCORE (RADIO)

A BBC production for BBC Radio 2. Transmission details are for BBC Radio 2. Usual duration: 28 minutes.
SERIES 2
Season credit(s):   Compiled by Richard Willcox; production by Richard Willcox.
Season performer(s): With Pete Murray (Chairman), Tony Blackburn (Team Captain), Terry Wogan (Team
                      Captain).

Holding / Source

27.02.1974 19:02 – 19:30 **Programme 37**   J / AA
With Neil Sedaka, Dickie Henderson.

06.03.1974 19:02 – 19:30 **Programme 38**   J / AA
With Bernard Cribbins, Dickie Henderson.

A PRESENT FOR DICKIE

A Thames Television production. Transmission details are for the ATV midlands region. Duration: 25 minutes.

Programme credit(s):   Devised by Jimmy Grafton; music by Ronnie Aldrich; designed by Roger Allan and Michael Minas; produced and directed by Peter Frazer-Jones.

Programme cast: Dickie Henderson (Dickie), Fabia Drake (Mother-in-Law, Mrs Upshott-Mainwaring), Dennis Ramsden (Parker), Billy Burden (William), Mini the Elephant (Herself).

Holding / Source

30.12.1969 20:30 – 21:00   J / 2"
Alternative transmissions: 01.01.1970 19:00 – 19:30, postponed from 30.12.1969: Thames Television.
Written by Jimmy Grafton and Johnny Heward.
With Jerry Ram (Abul), Robert Raglan (Policeman), Ernest Bale (Customs Officer).

06.01.1970 20:30 – 21:00 **Things That Go Bump in the Night**   J / 2"
Alternative transmissions: 08.01.1970 19:00 – 19:30: Thames Television.
Written by Jimmy Grafton and Johnny Heward.
With Robert Raglan (Policeman).

13.01.1970 20:30 – 21:00 **Regina Versus Mini**   J / 2"
Alternative transmissions: 15.01.1970 19:00 – 19:30: Thames Television.
Written by Jimmy Grafton, Johnny Heward and Stan Mars.
With Jerry Ram (Abul), Robert Raglan (Policeman), John Rae (Magistrate), Bertie Hare (Clerk of the Court), Dickie Martyn (Drunk), Fay Bura (Traffic Warden), Dorothy Watson (Policewoman in Court), Kenneth Henry (Driver of Funeral Car), Marjorie Clarke (Mourner), Doris Hall (Mourner / Old Lady on Zebra Crossing), Pat Travis (Mourner).

20.01.1970 20:30 – 21:00 **Splash Headline**   J / 2"
Alternative transmissions: 22.01.1970 19:00 – 19:30: Thames Television.
Written by Jimmy Grafton and Johnny Heward.
With Jerry Ram (Abul), Myra Frances (Daphne Parkington).

27.01.1970 20:30 – 21:00 **Mini Golf**   J / 2"
Alternative transmissions: 29.01.1970 19:00 – 19:30: Thames Television.
Written by Jimmy Grafton, Johnny Heward and Stan Mars.
With Ted Ray (Himself).

03.02.1970 20:30 – 21:00 **Mini's Green Eye**   J / 2"
Alternative transmissions: 05.02.1970 19:00 – 19:30: Thames Television.
Written by Jimmy Grafton and Johnny Heward.
With June Laverick (Jane), Pete Murray (TV Host), David Hamilton (Newsreader), Laurie West (Weatherman), Gerry Tebbutt (Paul).

THE ROY CASTLE SHOW

A BBC production for BBC 1. Transmission details are for BBC 1.

Programme performer(s):   Roy Castle (Host).

SERIES 3

Duration: 45 minutes.

Season credit(s):   Script by Eric Davidson; musical director Ronnie Hazlehurst; choreography by Nita
                       Howard; designed by Vic Meredith; production by Michael Hurll.

Season performer(s): With Vince Hill, Berry Cornish, Laura Symonds, Eli Woods, Pat Lovett (Dancer), Wendy
                      Gotelee (Dancer), Anne Lewington (Dancer), Rosemary Clarke (Dancer), The
                      Breakaways (Vocal Backing).

Holding / Source

20.06.1970 20:15 – 21:00   R1 / 2"

With Dickie Henderson, Mary Hopkin, Jan Daley, Barry Alldis [as The Disc Jockey Band], Tony Blackburn [as
The Disc Jockey Band], Pete Drummond [as The Disc Jockey Band], Anne Nightingale [as The Disc Jockey
Band], Ed Stewart [as The Disc Jockey Band], Dave Lee Travis [as The Disc Jockey Band], Johnny Walker
[as The Disc Jockey Band], Vicki Murden (Dancer), Maureen Willsher (Dancer).

THE ROYAL VARIETY PERFORMANCE

An ITV Various production for ITV. Transmission details are for ITV.

Transmission details are for the ABC midlands region.

Holding / Source

10.11.1963   B-R1

An ATV production. Duration: 158 minutes.

Additional material by Ray Galton and Alan Simpson; orchestra conducted by Harold Collins; production
supervisor Bernard Delfont; directed for television by Bill Ward; directed for the stage by Robert Nesbitt.

With Dickie Henderson (Host), The Beatles, Wilfrid Brambell (Albert Steptoe), Harry H. Corbett (Harold
Steptoe), Marlene Dietrich, Charlie Drake, Michael Flanders and Donald Swann, Buddy Greco, Joe Loss and
his Orchestra, Nadia Nerina, Susan Maughan, Desmond Doyle, Christopher Newton, Keith Rosson, Ronald
Plaisted, Luis Alberto del Parana & Los Paraguayos, Harry Secombe, The cast of Pickwick, Tommy Steele,
The cast of Half A Sixpence, Eric Sykes & Hattie Jacques, The Clark Brothers, Francis Brunn, The Billy Petch
Dancers, Pinky and Perky, The Prince of Wales Theatre Orchestra.

Galton and Simpson were responsible for scripting the Steptoe and Son sketch, not the entire show.

19.11.1967 19:25 – 22:35   J

An ATV production. Duration: 150 minutes.

Presented by Bernard Delfont; musical director Billy Ternent; dances staged by Robert Nesbitt; designed by
Richard Lake; executive producer Bill Ward; directed for television by Albert Locke.

With Ken Dodd, Dickie Henderson, Tommy Cooper, Lulu, Harry Secombe, Rolf Harris, Vikki Carr, Bob Hope,
The Rockin' Berries, The Bluebell Girls, Val Doonican, Dougie Squires' Boys and Girls, Tom Jones, Mirielle
Mathieu, The Rumanian National Dance Company and Orchestra, Sandie Shaw, Tanya [Elephant], The
London Palladium Orchestra, The Bel Cantos.

Production Date(s): **Recording**: 13.11.1967 [London Palladium], 16.11.1967 [Captions - Elstree studio B]

There was a ten minute interval, from 21:25 to 21:35 while the evening news was broadcast.

THE ROYAL VARIETY PERFORMANCE

A BBC production. Transmission details are for BBC/BBC1.

Holding / Source

04.11.1962   R3

Duration: 180 minutes.

Dances staged by Robert Nesbitt; produced and directed by Duncan Wood.

With Raymond Baxter (Commentator), Edie Adams, The Black and White Minstrel Show, Rudy Cardenas, Rosemary Clooney, Johnny Dankworth and his Orchestra, Dickie Henderson, Bob Hope, Frank Ifield, Eartha Kitt, Cleo Laine, Palladium Girls and Boys, The Great Magyar Pusztai Troupe, Cliff Richard, Edmundo Ross and his Orchestra, Harry Secombe, The Shadows, Andy Stewart, Eric Sykes, Sophie Tucker, Norman Vaughan, Mike Winters, Bernie Winters.

05.11.1972 19:25 – 22:15   DB-D3 / 2"

Duration: 160 minutes.

Includes a Till Death Us Do Part sketch.

Presented by Bernard Delfont; dances staged by Robert Nesbitt; television presentation by Michael Hurll; additional direction by Dennis Main Wilson.

With Tom Fleming (Commentator), The Jackson Five, Liberace, Ken Dodd, Carol Channing, Elton John, Rod Hull and Emu, Jack Jones, Los Diablos Del Bombo, Dickie Henderson, Danny La Rue, The Trio Hoganas, Mike Yarwood, Warren Mitchell (Alf Garnett), Dandy Nichols (Else Garnett), Anthony Booth (Mike), The London Palladium Orchestra (Resident Orchestra).

A SANTA FOR CHRISTMAS

An ATV production. Transmission details are for the ATV midlands region. Duration: 75 minutes.

Written by Sid Colin and Jimmy Grafton; music associate Kenny Powell; dance direction by Eleanor Fazan; designed by Tom Lingwood and Tony Waller; executive producer Bill Ward; produced and directed by Brian Tesler.

Dickie Henderson, Joyce Blair, Joan Savage, The Eleanor Fazan Dancers, Jack Parnell and his Orchestra, Anthea Askey, Arthur Haynes, Arthur Askey, Tommy Cooper, Terry-Thomas, Avril Angers, Leslie Mitchell, Donald Gray, Diana Decker, William Hartnell, Geoffrey Sumner, Paddie O'Neil, Robin Bailey, Michael Miles, Hughie Green, David Jacobs, Irene Handl, Pat Coombs, Freddie Mills, Jack Solomons, Alfred Marks, Bill Owen, Danny Green, Len Harvey, Eric Boon, Kid Lewis, Billy Wells [as Bombardier Billy Wells], Dave Crowley, Val Parnell, Norman Wisdom, Johnnie Ray, Shani Wallis, Joan Regan, Rosemary Miller, Jill Browne, Charles Tingwell, Glyn Owen, Frederick Bartman.

Holding / Source

26.12.1957 21:00 – 22:30   R1N PO

Mute studio recording. 80 mins of retakes. Mainly musical routines that look like link pieces to the guests. It had such a great cast, but most are not present at all in the clips.

SATURDAY NIGHT IS GALA NIGHT (RADIO)

A BBC production for BBC Radio 2. Transmission details are for BBC Radio 2. Usual duration: 120 minutes.

Holding / Source

07.03.1981 20:00 – 22:00 **Roger Webb's World of Music / Dickie Henderson**   J / AAS

Introduced by Sarah Kennedy and David Hamilton; production by David Rayvern Allen.

With Roger Webb and his Orchestra, Danny Williams, Dickie Henderson, Diane Solomon, Cantabile, The Burt Rhodes Orchestra.

From the Golders Green Hippodrome. The two segments (Webb / Williams / Kennedy and Henderson, Solomon / Cantabile / Rhodes, Hamilton) were later repeated as separate programmes, 60 minutes each.

SATURDAY SHOW (RADIO)

A BBC production for BBC Home Service. Transmission details are for BBC Home Service.

	Holding / Source
30.10.1954 13:10 – 14:10	NR / Live

Show band directed by Cyril Stapleton; production by Johnnie Stewart.

With Dickie Henderson, Dickie Valentine, Rikki Fulton, The Stargazers, Bill McGuffie, Bert Weedon, Harold Smart, The Show Band Singers, BBC Show Band.

SATURDAY SHOWTIME

Produced for ITV by a variety of companies (see details below). Transmission details are for the ATV midlands region.

		Holding / Source
20.05.1978	**I'm Dickie – That's Showbusiness**	DB / 2"

An ATV production. Duration: 50 minutes.

Written by Dick Vosburgh and Garry Chambers; music by Jack Parnell and his Orchestra; designed by Tony Ferris; produced and directed by Paul Stewart Laing.

With Dickie Henderson (Host), Arthur Askey, Petula Clark, Michele Dotrice, Wayne Sleep, Roger Whittaker, Karen Kay, The Irving Davies Dancers, George Hamer Singers.

(VAL PARNELL'S) SATURDAY SPECTACULAR

An ATV production. Transmission details are for the ATV London region. Usual duration: 50 minutes.

	Holding / Source
19.01.1957 21:00 – 21:45 **The Dickie Henderson Show**	NR / Live

Designed by Charles Carroll; produced by Brian Tesler.

With Dickie Henderson, Shani Wallis.

	Holding / Source
06.04.1957 20:30 – 21:15 **Bernard Delfont Presents the Dickie Henderson Show**	NR / Live

Script by Dickie Henderson and Jimmy Grafton; choreography by Barbara Aitken; designed by Anthony Waller; produced and directed by Brian Tesler.

With Dickie Henderson, Jack Parnell and his Orchestra (Resident Orchestra), Jack Buchanan, The Tanner Sisters, The John Tiller Girls.

	Holding / Source
06.07.1957 21:30 – 22:30 **The Dickie Henderson Show**	NR|t / Live

Designed by Richard Lake; produced and directed by Brian Tesler.

With Dickie Henderson, Freddie Mills, Anthea Askey.

TV Times lists Albert Locke as producer/director and contemporary ATV paperwork suggests that this had been the original intention. The same paperwork indicates that the actual director was Brian Tesler, a fact confirmed beyond all reasonable doubt by the survival of a set of Telesnaps.

	Holding / Source
10.08.1957 21:30 – 22:30 **Bernard Delfont Presents The Dickie Henderson Show**	NR / Live

Designed by John Dinsdale and Richard R. Greenough; produced by Brian Tesler.

With Dickie Henderson, Freddie Mills, Anthea Askey, Jack Parnell and his Orchestra (Resident Orchestra), Dick Henderson.

	Holding / Source
30.11.1957 **Bernard Delfont Presents the Dickie Henderson Show**	R1 / LiveR1

Alternative transmissions: 03.12.1957: ATV Midlands.

Written by Alan Melville and Jimmy Grafton; designed by Tom Lingwood; produced and directed by Brian Tesler.

With Dickie Henderson, Freddie Mills, Anthea Askey, Diana Dors, The Malcolm Mitchell Trio, Jack Parnell and his Debonaires.

01.03.1958   **The Dickie Henderson Show: An Englishman in Paris**   R1 / LiveR1
Choreography by Lionel Blair; designed by Tom Lingwood; produced and directed by Brian Tesler.
With Dickie Henderson, Anthea Askey, Jack Parnell and his Orchestra (Resident Orchestra), The Confrey Phillips Trio, Freddie Phillips.

SATURDAY STARS

Produced for ITV by a variety of companies (see details below). Transmission details are for the ATV midlands region. Usual duration: 40 minutes.

Holding / Source

30.11.1968   **The Bachelors Show**   J
An ATV production.
With The Bachelors, Esther & Abi Ofarim, Dickie Henderson, The Clark Brothers, Tammy Jones.

SATURDAY VARIETY

An ATV production. Transmission details are for the ATV midlands region. Usual duration: 52 minutes.
Programme credit(s):   Music associate Derek Scott.
Programme performer(s):   Jack Parnell and his Orchestra (Resident Orchestra).

Holding / Source

08.04.1972   DB / 2"
Written by Bryan Blackburn and Barry Cryer; choreography by Dougie Squires; designed by Ken Wheatley; produced and directed by Colin Clews.
With Dickie Henderson, Lulu, Shari Lewis, Larry Grayson, The Pattersons, Dougie Squires' Second Generation, Des Lane*.

Performers marked as uncredited are not listed in TVTIMES but have been pulled in from other sources, most notably BFI's SIFT database.

SAY IT WITH MUSIC (RADIO)

A BBC production for BBC Light Programme. Transmission details are for BBC Light Programme.
SERIES 3

Holding / Source

29.01.1956 19:30 – 20:30   J / AA
Introduced by Jack Payne; orchestra conducted by Paul Fenoulhet; choir directed by George Mitchell; production by Glyn Jones.
With Vera Lynn, Dickie Henderson, Lizbeth Webb and Edmund Hockridge, Reub Silver and Marion Day, Robert Earl, The Londonaires, The Basil and Ivor Kirchin Band, The Mitchell Choristers, Augmented BBC Variety Orchestra.

SECOMBE AND FRIENDS

An ATV production. Transmission details are for the ABC midlands region. Usual duration: 50 minutes.
Programme performer(s):   Harry Secombe (Himself).

Holding / Source

21.05.1967   J / 40
Written by Jimmy Grafton; programme associate Jimmy Grafton; additional material by R. M. Hills and S. C. Green; orchestra conducted by Peter Knight; choreography by Lionel Blair; designed by Brian Bartholomew; produced and directed* by Jon Scoffield.
With Bruce Forsyth, Dickie Henderson, Patricia Kern, Bernard Miles.

SHARI'S SHOW

An LWT production. Transmission details are for the Anglia region. Duration: 25 minutes.

Programme credit(s):   Written by Jeremy Tarcher and Shari Lewis; designed by Martin Johnson; produced by Philip Casson.

Programme performer(s):   Shari Lewis (Host).

Holding / Source

20.03.1971 17:50 – 18:20 **Retirement**   2"|n / 62

Alternative transmissions: 28.02.1971 16:05 – 16:35: Westward Television; 12.09.1971 17:35 – 18:05: LWT. Directed by Philip Casson.

With Dickie Henderson, Ray Davis, Roz Early, Elaine Page, Dee Eldridge, Mark Brown, Bernard Sharpe.

SHOW BAND SHOW (RADIO)

A BBC production for BBC Light Programme. Transmission details are for BBC Light Programme.

Spotlighting the world of popular music.

SERIES 2

Holding / Source

24.09.1953 21:00 – 22:00   NR / Live

Introduced by Rikki Fulton; musical director Cyril Stapleton; production by Johnnie Stewart.

With Dickie Henderson, Bill McGuffie, Louis Stevens, BBC Show Band, Julie Dawn, Harold Smart, The Show Band Singers.

SHOW OF THE WEEK

A BBC production for BBC 2. Transmission details are for BBC 2.

Holding / Source

01.03.1966   **The Dickie Henderson Show**   R1

Duration: 45 minutes.

Written by Jimmy Grafton; choreography by Malcolm Goddard; designed by Mel Cornish; produced and directed by Michael Hurll.

With Dickie Henderson, Roy Castle, Brian Rix, The Clark Brothers, Dilys Watling, Georgina Moon, Sarah Maddern, The Malcolm Goddard Dancers, Ken Jones and his Orchestra.

22.04.1967   **Dickie Henderson**   J

Duration: 45 minutes.

Written by Robert Gray; orchestra directed by Alyn Ainsworth; choreography by Malcolm Goddard; designed by Robert Macgowan; produced and directed by Michael Hurll.

With Dickie Henderson, Adele Leigh, Leslie A. Hutchinson [as Hutch], The Peiro Brothers, The Clark Brothers, Len Lowe, Leslie Noyes, Georgina Moon, John Mulgrew, Bruce Wells, The Malcolm Goddard Dancers and Showgirls, The Fred Tomlinson Singers.

SHOWTIME

An ATV production. Transmission details are for CBS.

Holding / Source

19.07.1968   NP

With Phyllis Diller (Compere), The Shadows, Anita Harris, Michael Bentine, Frankie Vaughan, Dickie Henderson, The Five Luxors.

Source: The Big Show 05.05.1968

Re-edits of other ATV variety shows, mainly The Big Show, made and shown in the USA.

SOUTH COAST SPECIAL (RADIO)

A BBC production for BBC Radio 2. Transmission details are for BBC Radio 2. Duration: 75 minutes.

Dickie Henderson introduces some of the stars who are shining on the South Coast this summer.

Production by Brian Patten.

Dickie Henderson (Host), Frank Ifield, Terry Scott and Hugh Lloyd, Ivor Emmanuel, Semprini, Nancy Whiskey, The New Faces, The Eric Delaney Band, Michael Bentine.

Holding / Source

07.09.1968 19:35 – 20:50   J / AA

From the Winter Gardens, Bournemouth.

SPOTLIGHT

A BBC production for BBC 2. Transmission details are for BBC 2.

Programme credit(s):   Script associate Jimmy Perry; production by Don Sayer.

SERIES 1

Duration: 45 minutes.

Holding / Source

23.05.1983 21:40 – 22:25   DB / 1"

Dickie recounts some of the highlights of a long career in show business and illustrates with a song, a dance and hilarious impressions the style which has made him a top-class entertainer.

Music by The Gerry Collins Quartet; sound John Drake; lighting by Geoff Lomas.

With Dickie Henderson, Bertie Hare.

This interview was repeated on 09.10.1985 as a tribute to Dickie Henderson who had died on 22.09.1985.

STAR CHOICE (RADIO)

A BBC production for BBC Radio 2. Transmission details are for BBC Radio 2.

Holding / Source

01.12.1979 12:02 – 13:02   J / AAS

Production by Jack Dabbs.

With Dickie Henderson.

08.12.1979 12:02 – 13:02   J / AAS

Production by Jack Dabbs.

With Dickie Henderson.

15.12.1979 12:02 – 13:02   J / AAS

Production by Jack Dabbs.

With Dickie Henderson.

STAR LIGHT ENTERTAINMENT

An LWT production. Transmission details are for the ATV midlands region. Duration: 52 minutes.

Holding / Source

10.08.1968 20:20 – 21:20 **Meet José Ferrer**   J

Written by Eric Merriman; musical director Harry Rabinowitz; choreography by Paddy Stone; designed by Malcolm Middleton; associate producer Paddy Stone; produced and directed by Keith Beckett.

With Dickie Henderson, Adele Leigh, Bobby Vee, Don Partridge, Davy Kaye, The Paddy Stone Dancers, José Ferrer.

THE STARS ENTERTAIN

An Independent Television production for Thames Television. Transmission details are for the Central region. Duration: 100 minutes.

A tribute to Dickie Henderson OBE.

Script associate Barry Cryer; consultant Billy Marsh; musical director Harry Rabinowitz; choreography by Paddy Stone and Norman Maen; designed by David Marshall; associate producer Bridget Moore; produced by Louis Benjamin and Philip Jones; directed for television by Philip Casson; directed for the stage by Norman Maen.

Dickie Henderson (Subject of Tribute Programme), Mike Yarwood, Ernie Wise, Paul Gyngell, Diane Solomon, Lionel Jeffries, Bob Monkhouse, Noel Edmonds, Paul Nicholas, Jim Davidson, Jimmy Tarbuck, Leslie Crowther, Lionel Blair, Elaine Paige, Danielle Carson, Roy Castle, Windsor Davies, Louise English, Vince Hill, Hope and Keen, Tommy Korberg, Linda Lusardi, Julia McKenzie, Sir John Mills, Maggie Moone, Peter-Alex Newton, Peter Piper, Victor Ponce, Alan Price, Sir Anthony Quayle, Anneka Rice, Tim Rice, Anton Rodgers, Doreen Wells, June Whitfield, Iris Williams, Bernie Winters, Henry Cooper, Dickie Davies, Jack Douglas, William Franklyn, Peter Goodwright, Diane Hart, David Jacobs, Geoff Love, Aimi MacDonald, Pamela Manson, Alfred Marks, Jerry Stevens, Ed Stewart, Tony Venner, John Wade, Harry Worth, Neil Coles, Bernard Gallagher, Tommy Horton, Michael King, Bill Longmuir, The Show Dancers, The Stephen Hill Singers.

	Holding / Source
05.05.1986 20:00 – 22:00	1" / 1"

THE STARS SHINE FOR JACK

An ATV production. Transmission details are for the ABC midlands region. Duration: 75 minutes.

Introduced by Sir Malcolm Sargent; production supervisor Bernard Delfont; directed for television by Bill Ward; directed for the stage by Alec Shanks.

Dora Bryan, Eddie Calvert, Russ Conway, The Crazy Gang, Paul Daneman, Marlene Dietrich, Charlie Drake, Flanagan and Allen, Bruce Forsyth, Eileen Gourlay, Monsewer Eddie Gray, Dickie Henderson, David Johns and The Nocturns, Pat Kirkwood, Elizabeth Larner, Joe Loss and his Orchestra, Vera Lynn, Spike Milligan, Charlie Naughton, Nadia Nerina, Nervo and Knox, Peter O'Toole, Al Read, Billy Ternent and his Orchestra, The Barron Knights, The Tiller Girls, Sophie Tucker, Ted Shapiro, Albert and Les Ward, Tommy Trinder, Ted Ray, Cyril Dowler, Clarkson Rose, George Doonan, George Elrick, Ben Warriss, Bud Flanagan, Johnnie Risco, Georgie Wood, Arthur Scott, Charlie Chester.

	Holding / Source
30.05.1965	J / Live

In aid of the Jack Hylton Memorial Appeal. The production also included excerpts from the shows "Camelot", "Little Me" and "Maggie May".

STARSTRUCK (RADIO)

A BBC production for BBC Home Service. Transmission details are for BBC Home Service.

Programme credit(s):   Written by Bob Monkhouse and Denis Goodwin.

Programme cast: Bob Monkhouse, Denis Goodwin.

SERIES 2

	Holding / Source
16.04.1956 20:30 – 21:00 **A Salute to Showbusiness**	DA / AA

Production by John Hooper.

With Dickie Henderson, Annette Klooger, Nat Temple and his Orchestra.

VAL PARNELL'S SUNDAY NIGHT AT THE LONDON PALLADIUM

An ATV production. Transmission details are for ITV. Usual duration: 52 minutes.

SERIES 2
Transmission details are for the ABC midlands region.

An ITP production for ABC/ATV. Transmission details are for the ABC midlands region. Duration varies - see below for details.

Holding / Source

14.10.1956   J / Live

Orchestra directed by Eric Rogers; designed by Richard R. Greenough; produced by Val Parnell; directed by Bill Ward.

With Tommy Trinder (Compere), Liberace, The Beverley Sisters, Dickie Henderson, George Carden's London Palladium Girls, The London Palladium Orchestra.

SERIES 3
Transmission details are for the ABC midlands region.

Holding / Source

15.09.1957   J / Live

Produced by Val Parnell; directed by Brian Tesler.

With Dickie Henderson (Host), Harry Secombe, Shani Wallis, The Clarke Brothers, Sabrina, George Carden's London Palladium Girls, Cyril Ornadel and The London Palladium Orchestra.

22.09.1957   J / Live

Produced by Val Parnell; directed by Brian Tesler.

With Dickie Henderson (Host), Frankie Vaughan, The John Tiller Girls, Anne Shelton, Nadia Nerina, Alexis Rassine, Albert and Les Ward, Leo de Lyon, The King Brothers, Cyril Ornadel and The London Palladium Orchestra.

29.09.1957   J / Live

Executive producer Val Parnell; produced and directed by Brian Tesler.

With Dickie Henderson (Host), Jayne Mansfield, Allan Jones, George Carden's London Palladium Girls, Cyril Ornadel and The London Palladium Orchestra.

06.10.1957   J / Live

Executive producer Val Parnell; produced and directed by Brian Tesler.

With Georges Guetary, Juliette Greco, Dickie Henderson (Host), Bob Monkhouse, George Carden's London Palladium Girls, Cyril Ornadel and The London Palladium Orchestra.

20.10.1957   J / Live

Executive producer Val Parnell; produced and directed by Brian Tesler.

With Dickie Henderson (Guest Host), Bob Monkhouse (Billed as Host but was ill), Dave King, Shirley Bassey, Cyril Ornadel and The London Palladium Orchestra, The Tiller Girls.

Joan Regan was billed but replaced by Shirley Bassey.

02.02.1958   J / Live

Choreography by George Carden; executive producer Val Parnell; produced and directed by Brian Tesler.

With Dickie Henderson (Host), The Don Cossack Chorus And Dancers, Lenny the Lion with Terry Hall, Frankie Howerd, The Tiller Girls, Cyril Ornadel and The London Palladium Orchestra.

09.02.1958   J / Live

Choreography by George Carden; executive producer Val Parnell; produced and directed by Brian Tesler.

With Dickie Henderson (Host), Don Ameche, The Tiller Girls, The London Palladium Boys and Girls, Cyril Ornadel and The London Palladium Orchestra.

16.02.1958   R1SEQ / Live

Choreography by Barbara Aitken; dance direction by George Carden; executive producer Val Parnell; produced and directed by Brian Tesler.

With Dickie Henderson (Host), Max Bygraves, The Kaye Sisters, The Clark Brothers, The Tiller Girls, Cyril Ornadel and The London Palladium Orchestra.

Huntley have a 9 minute extract of this show as part of a promo film introduced by Ludovic Kennedy. It consists of the Kaye Sisters and then Singalongamax performing a song accompanied by loads of dancers.

23.02.1958   J / Live

Dance direction by George Carden; executive producer Val Parnell; produced and directed by Brian Tesler.

With Dickie Henderson (Host), Frankie Vaughan, Chic Murray, The London Palladium Boys and Girls, Cyril Ornadel and The London Palladium Orchestra.

16.03.1958   J / Live

Choreography by Barbara Aitken; dance direction by George Carden; executive producer Val Parnell; produced and directed by Brian Tesler.

With Frankie Howerd, Dickie Henderson (Host), The Beverley Sisters, Edmund Hockridge, Os Brasileros, The John Tiller Girls, Cyril Ornadel and The London Palladium Orchestra.

25.05.1958   J / Live

Choreography by Barbara Aitken; dance direction by George Carden; executive producer Val Parnell; produced by Brian Tesler.

With Dickie Henderson (Host), Max Bygraves, Joan Regan, The Rockets, The John Tiller Girls, Cyril Ornadel and The London Palladium Orchestra.

01.06.1958   J / Live

Dance direction by George Carden; executive producer Val Parnell; produced by Brian Tesler.

With Dickie Henderson (Host), Bob Crosby, Betty Kean, Lew Parker, Alma Cogan, The London Palladium Boys and Girls, Cyril Ornadel and The London Palladium Orchestra.

08.06.1958   J / Live

Choreography by Barbara Aitken; dance direction by George Carden; executive producer Val Parnell; produced by Brian Tesler.

With Dickie Henderson (Host), Vic Damone, Juanita Hall, Pinky and Perky, The John Tiller Girls, Cyril Ornadel and The London Palladium Orchestra.

15.06.1958   J / Live

Dance direction by George Carden; executive producer Val Parnell; produced by Brian Tesler.

With Dickie Henderson (Host), Marguerite Piazzi, Michael Medwin, Bernard Bresslaw, Norman Rossington, The London Palladium Boys and Girls, Cyril Ornadel and The London Palladium Orchestra.

SERIES 4

Transmission details are for the ABC midlands region.

Season performer(s): With Bruce Forsyth (Compere), Cyril Ornadel and The London Palladium Orchestra.

Holding / Source

11.01.1959   J / Live

Choreography by Barbara Aitken; dance direction by George Carden; designed by Tom Lingwood; executive producer Val Parnell; produced by Albert Locke.

With Dickie Henderson, Joni James, Freddie Mills, The Tiller Girls.

25.01.1959   J / Live

Choreography by Barbara Aitken; dance direction by George Carden; designed by Tom Lingwood; executive producer Val Parnell; produced by Albert Locke.

With Dickie Henderson, Rosemary June, Larry Griswold, The Tiller Girls.

SERIES 5

Transmission details are for the ABC midlands region.

Season credit(s): Executive producer Val Parnell.

Season performer(s): With Bruce Forsyth (Compere), Cyril Ornadel and The London Palladium Orchestra.

Holding / Source

24.01.1960 J / Live

Dance direction by Lionel Blair; designed by Richard R. Greenough; produced by Albert Locke.

With Dickie Henderson, June Laverick, Eleanor Summerfield, Frank Leighton, John Hewer, Leo Britt, Sarah Vaughan, The Tiller Girls.

Included an excerpt from the current theatre hit When In Rome, then playing at the Adelphi Theatre, London.

See also: SUNDAY NIGHT AT THE LONDON PALLADIUM

SUNDAY NIGHT AT THE LONDON PALLADIUM

An ATV production. Transmission details are for the ATV midlands region. Duration: 52 minutes.

Transmission details are for the ATV midlands region.

Season credit(s): Music associate Sam Harding.

Season performer(s): With Jack Parnell and his Orchestra.

Holding / Source

03.03.1974 J / 2"

Special material by Wally Malston; choreography by Dougie Squires; designed by Norman Smith; produced by Albert Locke; directed by John Pullen.

With Ted Rogers (Compere), Tony Bennett, Dickie Henderson, Dana, The Half Wits, Dougie Squires' Second Generation.

See also: VAL PARNELL'S SUNDAY NIGHT AT THE LONDON PALLADIUM

TARBUCK'S BACK

An ATV production. Transmission details are for the ATV midlands region. Duration: 25 minutes.

Programme credit(s): Written by Bryan Blackburn; additional material by Ron McDonnell; produced and directed* by Colin Clews.

Programme performer(s): Jimmy Tarbuck (Host), Jack Parnell and his Orchestra (Resident Orchestra), The Mike Sammes Singers (Resident Backing Singers).

Holding / Source

05.04.1968 20:30 – 21:00 DVSEQ / 2"

Alternative transmissions: 10.04.1968 19:00 – 19:30: Rediffusion Television.

Designed by Bryan Holgate.

With The Hollies, Audrey Jeans, Dickie Henderson, Rita Webb.

19 mins of this edition exists, ex-CV2000. The music numbers are in the main excluded.

TELL ME ANOTHER

A Southern Television production. Transmission details are for the ATV midlands region. Duration: 25 minutes.

Programme performer(s): Dick Hills (Host).

SERIES 4

Season credit(s): Directed by John Coxall and Paul Bryers.

Holding / Source

01.07.1980 "The day they made their first big break, and the days DB / 2"
they didn't"

With Derek Batey, Dickie Henderson, Vince Hill, Moira Lister, Peggy Mount, Tom O'Connor, Sylvia Syms, Norman Wisdom.

TELL ME ANOTHER (continued)

22.07.1980	"Favourite Showbiz Personalities"	DB / 2"

With Dickie Henderson, John Junkin, Roy Kinnear, Moira Lister, Cliff Michelmore, Peggy Mount, Tom O'Connor, Sydney Tafler.

19.08.1980	"Recognition"	DB / 2"

With Derek Batey, Roger de Courcey, Percy Edwards, Fred Emney, Dickie Henderson, John Junkin, Moira Lister, Cliff Michelmore, Peggy Mount, Cardew Robinson, Sydney Tafler, Tommy Trinder.

26.08.1980	"Spare Time"	DB / 2"

With Derek Batey, Acker Bilk, Leslie Crowther, Roger de Courcey, Charlie Drake, Fred Emney, Dickie Henderson, Dave Lee Travis, Tommy Trinder.

THEY SAID THIS?

A Border Television production. Transmission details are for border region. Duration: 23 minutes.

Programme credit(s): Produced by John Harkins.

Programme performer(s): Jim Bowen (Host), Derek Batey (Interviewer).

SERIES 2

Holding / Source

10.07.2003	DB

With Frank Carson, Ken Dodd, Barry Cryer, Norman Collier, Norman Vaughan, Tom O'Connor, Stan Boardman, Tommy Trinder, Dickie Henderson, Little and Large, Mike and Bernie Winters, Ernie Wise, Ben Warriss, Jimmy Jewel, Les Dennis, Dustin Gee, Lennie Bennett, Kenny Cantor, Eddie Cantor, Kenneth Williams, Diana Dors.

24.07.2003	DB

With Jack Douglas, Barbara Windsor, Norman Wisdom, Mike and Bernie Winters, Diana Dors, William Franklyn, Dora Bryan, Ernie Wise, Bill Maynard, Jimmy Jewel, Dickie Henderson, Ted Rogers, Tommy Trinder, Noele Gordon, Stan Boardman.

Jim Bowen introduces clips from the LOOK WHO'S TALKING archive.

See also: LOOK WHO'S TALKING

THIS ENGLAND

A Granada production. Transmission details are for the Granada region.

Holding / Source

19.12.1977	**House of the Stars**	DB / C1

'Astra House' – House of the Stars. The digs used by stars near Northern Music Hall.

Film camera Mike Thomson; film editor Dai Vaughan; executive producer Norman Swallow; directed by Michael Darlow.

With Arthur Askey (Interviewee), Dickie Henderson (Interviewee), Ursula Howells (Interviewee), Alma McKay (Interviewee).

THIS IS YOUR LIFE

Produced for BBC/ITV by a variety of companies (see details below). Usual duration: 25 minutes.

Programme credit(s): Devised by Ralph Edwards.

SERIES 11

A Thames Television production. Transmission details are for the ATV midlands region.

Season credit(s): Produced by Robert Tyrell; directed by Margery Baker.

Season performer(s): With Eamonn Andrews (Presenter).

Holding / Source

17.02.1971	**Dickie Henderson**	J / 2"

With Dickie Henderson.

SERIES 22

A Thames Television production. Transmission details are for the ATV/Central region.

Season credit(s): Written by Tom Brennand and Roy Bottomley; programme associate Maurice Leonard; programme consultants Tom Brennand and Roy Bottomley; produced by Jack Crawshaw; directed by Terry Yarwood and Paul Stewart Laing.

Season performer(s): With Eamonn Andrews (Presenter).

Holding / Source

10.02.1982   **Bob Monkhouse**   DB-D3 / 2"

Created by Ralph Edwards; written by Tom Brennand and Roy Bottomley; programme associate Maurice Leonard; programme consultants Tom Brennand and Roy Bottomley; produced by Jack Crawshaw; directed by Paul Stewart Laing.

With Bob Monkhouse, Jackie Monkhouse, Abigail Monkhouse, Simon Monkhouse, Gary Monkhouse, Edith Ashby, Dickie Henderson, Arthur Mullard, Michele Dotrice, Pat Coombs, Denis Gifford, Diana Dors, Bob Hope, Liberace, Charlie Drake, June Whitfield, Dennis Main Wilson, Max Wall.

THIS IS YOUR LUNCH

A BBC production for BBC 1. Transmission details are for BBC 1.

Holding / Source

02.06.1971 19:00 – 19:30 **Harry Secombe**   DB-D3 / 2"

Duration: 30 minutes.

Alternative transmissions: 11.05.1971 22:10 – 22:40: BBC 1 London.

The Variety Club of Great Britain pays tribute to King Buffoon and memorable goon, Harry Secombe CBE, at a lunch celebrating his 25 years in show business.

Commentary by Keith Fordyce; television presentation by Philip Lewis.

With Harry Secombe, Jimmy Edwards, Eric Sykes, Dickie Henderson, Jimmy Tarbuck, Spike Milligan, Rt Hon Harold Wilson, Percy Livingstone.

The broadcast in May 1971 was to the London, Wales and Scotland regions only. In June 1971, the programme was fully networked.

THREE LIVE WIRES

Alternative/Working Title(s): THE MICHAEL MEDWIN SHOW

An Associated-Rediffusion production. Transmission details are for the ATV midlands region. Duration: 25 minutes.

Programme cast: Michael Medwin (Mike Lane), Bernard Fox (Malcolm Danders), George Roderick (George Smithers), Derek Benfield (Higgenbottom).

Holding / Source

03.07.1961   **Falling Star**   J / 40

Written by James Kelly and Peter Miller; designed by Frank Gillman; directed by Christopher Hodson.

With Deryck Guyler (Mr Farnum), Lionel Murton, Ronnie Stevens, Harry Littlewood, Joe Ritchie, Dickie Henderson.

Production Date(s): **Recording**: 28.04.1961

TOAST OF THE TOWN (RADIO)

A BBC production for BBC Home Service. Transmission details are for BBC Home Service.

Holding / Source

26.12.1957 21:15 – 22:00 **Christmas Edition**   J / AA

Devised by Trafford Whitelock; orchestra conducted by Harry Rabinowitz; produced by Trafford Whitelock.

With Eamonn Andrews (Host), Jim Dale, Dickie Henderson, Joan Sutherland, David Tomlinson, Anna Massey, Janet Blair, George Gaynes, The George Mitchell Singers, BBC Revue Orchestra.

THE VAL DOONICAN MUSIC SHOW

A BBC production for BBC 1. Transmission details are for BBC 1.

Programme performer(s): Val Doonican (Host).

Holding / Source

28.12.1981 21:10 – 21:55 **Val Sings Bing**   DB-D3 / 2"

Duration: 45 minutes.

Written by Benny Green and Val Doonican; musical director Ronnie Hazlehurst; music associate Roger Richards; sound Keith Gunn; lighting by Ken Macgregor; costume Laura Ergis; designed by Jan Spoczynski; produced and directed by Yvonne Littlewood.

With Vic Damone, Marti Webb, Dickie Henderson, Rosemarie Ford, Tracey Miller, Vicky Silva, Val Stokes, Penny Lister, Danny Street, Nick Curtis, Ken Barrie, John Evans, Jane Danielle, Camilla Blair, Victoria Shellard, Julie Dean.

THE VAL DOONICAN SHOW

An ATV production. Transmission details are for the ATV midlands region. Usual duration: 52 minutes.

Programme performer(s): Val Doonican (Host).

SERIES 4

Holding / Source

03.03.1973   DB / LivePAL

Written by David Cumming; choreography by Norman Maen; designed by Lewis Logan; produced and directed by Alan Tarrant.

With Lena Martell, Stéphane Grapelli, Dickie Henderson, The Norman Maen Dancers, Kenny Woodman and his Orchestra, Fabric.

Production Date(s): **Recording**: 02.03.1973 [Elstree studio D]; **Live Performance**: 03.03.1973 [Elstree studio D]

THE VAL DOONICAN SHOW

A BBC production for BBC 1. Transmission details are for BBC 1. Duration: 50 minutes.

Written by Spike Mullins and Val Doonican; musical director Kenny Woodman; choreography by Nigel Lythgoe; designed by Robin Tarsnane; produced by John Ammonds; directed by Stanley Appel.

Val Doonican (Host), José Feliciano, Diane Solomon, Dickie Henderson, The Nigel Lythgoe Dancers.

Holding / Source

24.05.1975 21:00 – 21:50   DB / 2"

THE VARIETY CLUB TRIBUTE DINNER TO MORECAMBE AND WISE

An ATV production. Transmission details are for the ATV midlands region. Duration: 25 minutes.

Designed by Tom Carter; produced and directed by John Pullen.

Terry Wogan (Host), Morecambe and Wise (Themselves), Leslie Crowther (Guest at Event), Maudie Edwards (Guest at Event), Dickie Henderson (Guest at Event), Aimi MacDonald (Guest at Event), Derek Nimmo (Guest at Event), George Elrick (Guest at Event), Noele Gordon (Guest at Event), Dora Bryan (Guest at Event), Glenda Jackson (Guest at Event), Larry Grayson (Guest at Event), Terry Hall and Lenny the Lion (Guest at Event).

Holding / Source

12.12.1978   DB / 2"

VARIETY FANFARE (RADIO)

A BBC production for BBC Light Programme. Transmission details are for BBC Light Programme. Usual duration: 45 minutes.

SERIES 4

Holding / Source

06.03.1953 20:00 – 20:45 **Programme 49**   J / AA
A BBC Manchester production.
Introduced by Alan Clarke; orchestra conducted by Vilem Tausky; production by Ronnie Taylor.

With The Kordites, Kirk Stevens, Dickie Henderson [as Dick Henderson Jnr], Rawicz and Landauer, Benny Hill, Muriel Smith, Robb Wilton, The Augmented Northern Variety Orchestra.

SERIES 5

Holding / Source

20.11.1953 19:30 – 20:15 **Programme 6**   J / AA
Introduced by Alan Clarke; orchestra conducted by Vilem Tausky; production by Ronnie Taylor.

With Norman George and his Violin, Littlewoods Girls' Choir, Dickie Henderson, Les Ward, Gladys Morgan, Lee Lawrence, Derek Roy, Rawicz and Landauer, The Kordites, The Augmented N.D.O..

VARIETY PLAYHOUSE (RADIO)

A BBC production for BBC Home Service. Transmission details are for BBC Home Service. Duration: 60 minutes.

A mixture of musical acts, and sketches, with a short play (or an excerpt from a longer one) thrown in.

SERIES 1

Holding / Source

23.05.1953 20:00 – 21:00   J
Orchestra conducted by Harry Rabinowitz; music adviser Vic Oliver; continuity by Carey Edwards; production by Tom Ronald.

With Vic Oliver (Host), Dickie Henderson [as Dickie Henderson Jnr], Gladys Ripley, Harry Locke, Judy Campbell, Bruce Trent, Terry-Thomas, The George Mitchell Choir, Augmented BBC Revue Orchestra.

17.10.1953 20:00 – 21:00   J
Orchestra conducted by Philip Martell and Vic Oliver; continuity by Carey Edwards; production by Tom Ronald.

With Vic Oliver (Host), Dick Bentley, Dickie Henderson, Marjorie Holt, Harry Locke, Marion Lowe, Tom Round, Ken Smith, Diana Wynyard, The George Mitchell Choir, Variety Concert Orchestra.

06.03.1954 20:00 – 21:00   J / AA
Orchestra conducted by Philip Martell and Vic Oliver; continuity by Carey Edwards; production by Tom Ronald.

With Vic Oliver (Host), Max Geldray, Dickie Henderson, Harry Jacobson, Amy Shuard, Isabelle Cooley, Lance Taylor, Ken Freeman, Bee Freeman, The George Mitchell Choir, Variety Concert Orchestra.

06.11.1954 20:00 – 21:00   J / AA
Orchestra conducted by Vic Oliver and Philip Martell; continuity by Carey Edwards; production by Tom Ronald.

With Vic Oliver (Host), Eric Barker, Dickie Henderson, Robertson Hare, Ralph Lynn, Reginald Collin, Joanna Gay, Alex Finter, Billy Maxam, Robert Thomas, Victoria Sladen, Dickie Valentine, The George Mitchell Choir, The British Concert Orchestra.

02.04.1955 20:00 – 21:00   J / AA
Orchestra conducted by Vic Oliver and Philip Martell; continuity by Carey Edwards; production by Tom Ronald.

With Vic Oliver (Host), Kay Cavendish, Dickie Henderson, John Horvelle, Vanessa Lee, Derek Roy, Leslie Welch, The George Mitchell Choir, The British Concert Orchestra.

24.09.1955 20:00 – 21:00   J / AA
Production by John Simmonds.

With Kenneth Horne (Host), Richard Murdoch, John Hanson, Dickie Henderson, Julie Dawn, Reub Silver and Marion Day, The Marilyn Sisters, The Peter Knight Singers, Ron Goodwin and his Concert Orchestra.

22.10.1955 20:00 – 21:00   J
Orchestra conducted by Vic Oliver and Philip Martell; continuity by Carey Edwards; production by Tom Ronald.

With Vic Oliver (Host), Sylvia Campbell, Cyril Fletcher, Rawicz and Landauer, Dickie Henderson, Frederick Sharpe and Marjorie Shires, Bernard Spear, The George Mitchell Choir, The British Concert Orchestra.

26.11.1955 20:00 – 21:00   J
Conceived by Carey Edwards; orchestra conducted by Vic Oliver and Philip Martell; production by Tom

With Vic Oliver (Host), Albert and Les Ward, Dickie Henderson, Barbara Lyon, Robert Simmons, Bransby Williams, Vanda Vale, The George Mitchell Choir, The British Concert Orchestra.

07.04.1956 20:00 – 21:00   J
With Vic Oliver (Host), Eddie Calvert, Charlie Chester, Hubert Gregg, Dickie Henderson, Rosina Raisbeck.

SERIES 6

Season credit(s):   Written by Johnny Speight and Ernest Dudley; continuity by Carey Edwards; production by Alastair Scott-Johnston.

Season performer(s): With Vic Oliver (Host), BBC Revue Orchestra, The George Mitchell Choir, Ernest Dudley (Vic in a Spot Host / hat Would You Do? Host).

Holding / Source

02.05.1959 20:00 – 21:00 **The Trials of Life – Going to a Party / What Would You**   J
Do? – The Knife Thrower
With Cardew Robinson, Stanley Unwin, Howell Glynne, Vic Oliver (Himself), Patricia Hayes (Woman), Ronnie Barker (First Man), Tenniel Evans (Second Man), Michael Bates (Third Man), Tenniel Evans (Stage-Door Keeper), Ronnie Barker (Pete), Patricia Hayes (Karla), Michael Bates (Ed), Doreen Murray, Rowland Jones, Dickie Henderson.

SERIES 7

Season credit(s):   Play written by Gavin Blakeney; incidental music by Philip Martell; continuity by Carey Edwards; production by Alastair Scott-Johnston.

Season performer(s): With Vic Oliver (Host), Variety Playhouse Orchestra, The George Mitchell Choir.

Holding / Source

16.01.1960 20:00 – 21:00   J
Play written by Gavin Blakeney; incidental music by Philip Martell; orchestra conducted by Vic Oliver; continuity by Carey Edwards; produced by Alastair Scott-Johnston.

With Vic Oliver (Host), Cicely Courtneidge, Jack Hulbert, Robert Thomas, Victoria Elliott, Michael Langdon, The George Mitchell Choir, Chris Carlsen, Dickie Henderson, The Variety Playhouse Orchestra.

VARIETY ROAD SHOW (RADIO)

A BBC production for BBC Home Service. Transmission details are for BBC Home Service.

Holding / Source

02.09.1952 12:25 – 12:55   J / AA
Radio presentation by Eddie Fraser.

With Jack Radcliffe, Joan Mann, Dickie Henderson [as Dickie Henderson, Jnr.], The Teen-Agers, The Alan Stewart Quartet.

From the R.A.F. Station, Leuchars, Fife.

THE VIC OLIVER STORY (RADIO)

A BBC production for BBC Home Service. Transmission details are for BBC Home Service.

Narrated by Ben Lyon; written by Gale Pedrick; orchestra directed by Harry Rabinowitz; edited by Michael North; production by Michael North.

Bebe Daniels, Dickie Henderson, Pat Kirkwood, Henry Sherek, Vanda Vale, Peter Villes, Lord Willoughby de Broke, Vic Oliver, Barbara Leigh, The George Mitchell Singers, BBC Revue Orchestra.

	Holding / Source
26.09.1960 19:30 – 20:30	J / AA

THE WAY OF LIFE (RADIO)

A BBC production for BBC Home Service. Transmission details are for BBC Home Service.

Christians think about their faith.

	Holding / Source
20.04.1958 19:45 – 20:25 **The Church and the Showgirl**	J / AA

Introduced by Harold Rogers.

With The Reverend Vernon Mitchell, Pat Cochran, Vicky Grey, Anita Mann, Pat Newson, Dorothy Penny, June Reynolds, Petula Clark, Dickie Henderson.

WEEKEND

A Granada production. Transmission details are for the Granada region. Duration: 50 minutes.

SERIES 2

Season credit(s):   Produced by Geoff Moore.

	Holding / Source
22.02.1985	1" / 1"

Directed by Lorne Magory.

With Susie Mathis (Presenter), Ted Robbins (Presenter), Lennie Bennett, Dickie Henderson, Pauline Daniels.

WINNER TAKES ALL

A Yorkshire Television production. Transmission details are for the ATV midlands region. Usual duration: 25 minutes.

General knowledge gambling game.

Programme credit(s):   Devised by Geoffrey Wheeler; executive producer Lawrie Higgins.

Transmission details are for the ATV midlands region.

	Holding / Source
30.12.1978 18:15 – 18:45 **All Star Winner Takes All**	1" / 2"

Jimmy Tarbuck hosts a special edition of this popular quiz in which finalists gamble on their general knowledge with money from a £50 stake.

Questions set by Deborah Sutherland; designed by Roy Coldrick; executive producer Lawrie Higgins; produced and directed by Guy Caplin.

With Jimmy Tarbuck (Presenter), Geoffrey Wheeler (Voice Only), Moira Anderson, Henry Cooper, Anita Harris, Dickie Henderson.

Transmission details are for the ATV midlands region.

Holding / Source

26.12.1979 17:45 – 18:15 **All Star Winner Takes All**   1" / 2"

A seasonal edition of this quiz in which contestants gamble on their general knowledge. Host Jimmy Tarbuck takes the bets, and Geoffrey Wheeler puts the questions. The celebrity competitors — Moira Anderson, Anita Harris, Henry Cooper and Dickie Henderson — battle to win up to £1,000 for charity.

Written by Lawrie Kinsley and Ron McDonnell; questions set by Deborah Sutherland; designed by Roy Coldrick; executive producer Lawrie Higgins; produced and directed by Guy Caplin.

With Jimmy Tarbuck (Presenter), Geoffrey Wheeler (Voice Only), Moira Anderson, Anita Harris, Henry Cooper, Dickie Henderson.

WORKERS' PLAYTIME (RADIO)

A BBC production. Transmission details are for BBC Radio various.

Transmission details are for BBC Home Service.

Holding / Source

30.10.1952 12:25 – 12:55   J

Pianos Harry Carmichael and George Bowie; radio presentation by Howard M. Lockhart.

With Dickie Henderson, Joan Mann, Ike Freedman, Allen Christie.

From a jute factory in Dundee.

A WORLD OF MUSIC

A BBC production for BBC 2. Transmission details are for BBC 2.

SERIES 1

Holding / Source

10.12.1976 21:30 – 22:25 **Another Opening, Another Show**   DB-D3 / 2"

Musical director Peter Knight; music associate Ray Holder; staged by Gillian Lynne; sound Hugh Barker; lighting by Ken Macgregor; costume L. Rowland Warne; designed by Valerie Warrender; production by Yvonne Littlewood.

With John Mills, Dickie Henderson, Jessie Matthews, Barbara Mullen, Richard Murdoch, Anna Neagle, Cicely Courtneidge, Jack Hulbert, The Gillian Lynne Dancers, The Eddie Lester Singers.

YES! IT'S GREAT YARMOUTH! (RADIO)

A BBC production for BBC Light Programme. Transmission details are for BBC Light Programme.

Stars introduce some of the artists entertaining Yarmouth holiday-makers during the summer.

Holding / Source

10.09.1966 19:30 – 20:30   J / AA

Production by Richard Maddock.

With Dickie Henderson (Host), Donald Peers, The Barron Knights, Hope and Keen, The Shepherd Singers, Bert Edgar, The Karl Denver Trio, The Jackie Brown Orchestra.

Recorded at the Wellington Pier Pavilion.

YOUNG AND FOOLISH

An ATV production. Transmission details are for the ABC midlands region. Duration: 40 minutes.

A new song, fun and dance show with a continuing story about a band under the leadership of Jack Parnell. The band's financial backer is Mr Penny, played by Chic Murray while the band's manager was supposed to be played by Dickie Henderson but he left the production and was replaced in programme 2 by Michael Bentine and in programmes 3 and 4 by Bonar Colleano.

Programme credit(s):   Written by Bill Craig and John Law; designed by Anthony Waller; production by Dicky Leeman.

Holding / Source

06.10.1956 21:00 – 21:45   J / Live

With Chic Murray (Mr Penny), Jack Parnell, Dickie Henderson, Michael Holliday, Maidie Dickson (Mr Penny's Secretary), Tonia Bern, The Jack Parnell Orchestra.

Production Date(s): **Live Performance**: 06.10.1956 [Wood Green]

Although billed each week in TV Times, Dickie Henderson did not appear after the first programme.

HOLDING AND SOURCE FORMAT CODES AND DESCRIPTIONS

1"	625 line PAL colour 1" videotape.
1"-R1	625 line monochrome 1" videotape from 16mm monochrome telerecording
2"	625 line PAL colour 2" videotape.
40	405 line monochrome 2" videotape.
62	625 line monochrome 2" videotape.
AA	Analogue Audio.
AAS	Analogue Audio - Stereo.
B	Betacam SP videotape.
B-R1	Betacam SP videotape taken from 16mm monochrome telerecording.
C1	16mm colour film.
D2	D2 digital videotape.
D3	D3 digital videotape.
D3-R1	D3 digital videotape from 16mm monochrome telerecording.
DA	Digital Audio.
DB	Digital Betacam videotape.
DB-1"	Digital Betacam videotape taken from 625 line PAL colour 1" videotape.
DB-4W	Digital Betacam videotape copy of converted 405 to 625 line monochrome videotape.
DB-D3	Digital Betacam copy of a D3 digital videotape.
DB-NP	Digital Betacam videotape taken from 625 line PAL colour 2" videotape conversion of 525 line NTSC colour 2" videotape.
DB-R1	Digital Betacam videotape taken from 16mm monochrome film recording.
DB-R3	Digital Betacam videotape taken from 35mm monochrome film recording.
DV	625 line PAL domestic format videotape including VHS, Betamax and Philip 1500.
HD-R1	High Definition videotape taken from 16mm monochrome film telerecording (reverse anamorphic)
J	Does not exist.
Live	Live transmission.
Live40	Live transmission - recorded onto 405 line monochrome videotape off air.
LivePAL	Live transmission - recorded onto 625 line PAL colour videotape off air.
LiveR1	Live transmission - telerecorded onto 16mm monochrome film off air.
NM	Not made
NP	625 line PAL colour 2" videotape from 525 line NTSC colour 2" videotape.
NR	Not Recorded.
R1	16mm monochrome film telerecorded from 405/625 line videotape or a live transmission.
R3	35mm monochrome film telerecorded from 405/625 line videotape or a live broadcast.
UM	625 line U-Matic videotape copy.

ADDITIONAL FORMAT CODES

|a - Held on Domestic Audio

|n - Held at NFTVA

|t - Holding Telesnap

N - Only survives as film negative

PO - Picture only (no sound survives)

SEQ - Although the complete programme is missing, some sequences survive

L - #0138 - 080823 - C0 - 229/152/5 - PB - DID3653451